COSTUME of the ORIGINAL INHABITANTS of the BRITISH ISLANDS. &c. &c.

C.H.S. delt.

Aquatinted by R. Havell.

ANCIENT COSTUMES

OF

GREAT BRITAIN AND IRELAND,

FROM THE DRUIDS TO THE TUDORS

BY

CHARLES HAMILTON SMITH, ESQ.

Introduction by Doreen Yarwood

BRACKEN BOOKS
LONDON

Ancient Costumes of Great Britain and Ireland
was originally published in two volumes in 1814

This edition published by Bracken Books,
an imprint of Bestseller Publications Ltd.
Princess House, 50 Eastcastle Street
London W1N 7AP
ENGLAND

Copyright © 1989 Bracken Books

ISBN 1 85170 253 9

Printed in Italy

CONTENTS

Antient
Costume
of
England

INTRODUCTION

This book combines the two volumes devoted to the dress of the inhabitants of the British Isles, from 'earliest times' to AD 1500, which were the work of Charles Hamilton Smith and were first published in 1821. Both volumes were copiously illustrated by colour engravings, produced by a talented artist, which vividly depict not only the dress of the time but also the relevant backgrounds and artefacts. In text and illustrations this is more than a costume history; it is also of considerable social value. Among the subjects described and drawn are armies, battles and weapons, ships and tournaments, as well as more everyday pursuits such as fishing, archery and husbandry. In addition to fashionable dress, consideration is also given to the clothes worn by ordinary people, as well as to ecclesiastical costume and armour.

Apart from the interest aroused by the general attractiveness of such colour plates and the wealth of detailed information, it is never easy to evaluate such a work for the present-day reader. Mr Hamilton Smith did not have at his disposal, as has the modern costume historian, the wealth of reliable data which has become available since the 1820s from archaeological research and more recently discovered documentation. Yet it is interesting and encouraging to find that he has relied, particularly for the very early centuries, upon the same literary sources as we would use. He has drawn extensively on the accounts of Strabo, the Greek philosopher and historian who was born c.64 BC. Strabo travelled widely in Europe and the Middle East, recording his knowledge gained there in a seventeen-volume *Geography*, eight books of which were devoted to Europe.

For the almost five centuries of the Roman occupation of Britain, the author has relied heavily upon the numerous reports from Roman administrators, historians and writers, notably Caesar, Tacitus, Pliny the Elder, Dio Cassius and the Greek historian Diodorus Siculus for the early centuries, and Sidonius Apollinaris and Agathius in the later years. The impressions given by Caesar and Tacitus, in particular, are vivid and detailed. To Caesar and Strabo we owe much of our background understanding of the position of the Druids in society (though we know almost nothing of their dress), and from both Caesar and Tacitus there are detailed descriptions of the peoples of Britain and Gaul, their garments, fabrics, way of life and manner of waging war. The Penguin paperback edition of some of Tacitus' monographs, notably his *The Agricola and The Germania* (first published AD 98 and now reprinted 1971), has brought his clearly written account to the notice of many interested readers. Cornelius Tacitus was born in AD 56. His writings, taken together with the relief sculpture upon the two triumphal columns of Trajan (AD 114) and Marcus Aurelius (AD 174) which still stand in Rome, give a fairly comprehensive picture of dress in the northern, outer limits of the Roman Empire at this time.

The great distinction, however, between the use of these accounts by Hamilton Smith and by a modern historian is that the former had to rely almost entirely upon such evidence for his illustrative and textual material, whereas today we can check the description from more material evidence now available to us. The author of this work accepts uncritically those classical descriptions as he also does biblical statements from the Old Testament, for example 'that the descendants of Cain discovered metallurgy', or the relationship between the origins of Druidism and Noah.

Even as late as the early decades of the twentieth century it was still accepted that the 'Dark Ages' extended from the departure of the Roman legions from our shores in the fifth century almost to the arrival of William Duke of Normandy in 1066. Since then the 'Dark Ages' have become appreciably less dark, and archaeological excavation has given us a much clearer picture of this entire period. In dress, we are able to view in the Danish National Museum in Copenhagen and in the Schleswig-Holstein Prehistory Museum actual garments dating from the Bronze and Iron Ages which were found between the 1880s and 1930s, in a remarkable state of preservation, in the peat bogs of Denmark, northern Holland and Germany. Much later, medieval, examples have been discovered, similarly preserved, in Scottish peat areas. From further research and wider reading we have now learned to treat the classical records with a certain reserve and scepticism, as many of them are versions of earlier descriptions rewritten by authors who lived many years later and could not have viewed the scenes at first hand. This applies, for example, to Tacitus' account of Britons preparing to do battle with the Romans at the Menai Straits between Wales and Anglesey: the historian was a small boy at the time. The same must be true of the detailed account of Boadicea (Boudicca), Queen of the Iceni, arrayed for battle, written by the Roman historian Cassius Dio Cocceianus over 100 years after the event.

The second volume of Hamilton Smith's work provides much the greater proportion of this book, and covers the dress of Great Britain and Ireland from AD 750–1500. With more original material available for this period, at least from the twelfth century onwards, in the form of illuminated manuscripts, sculpture, coloured glass and paintings, the author has been able to give the authority from which he has derived the material for his text and illustration at the end of each appropriate page of text. He states that in many instances he has altered the pose of the figure(s) but has adhered faithfully to the dress style. Such changes of pose and form have provoked criticism from present-day historians in that, in this way, a true picture of the period may be partially lost, especially where the original authority has not been stated, a custom normal prior to the 1950s. However, where, as in this case, the source of the knowledge is clearly printed, any student of dress may compare the book version with the original source.

Suitable backgrounds are drawn for the majority of illustration pages. In some cases these consist of actual buildings appropriate to the time or landscapes and seascapes suited to the activities of boating, fishing or hunting. All of these backgrounds are accurately depicted, as are, for example, the ships of the Norman fleet of Duke William approaching the English shores in 1066, which have been carefully engraved from those embroidered on the Bayeux Tapestry (page 106). In a number of instances the author refers to the background as being 'ideal'. This seems to mean that a suitable one has been supplied which is not based upon a specific original.

Mr. Hamilton Smith has gone to great pains to make the illustrations as accurate as possible. It is amusing, though, to read on page 123 (Avelina, Countess of Lancaster) that the artist was so careful in making sure that he obtained a correct colouring for the lady's robes that he scraped some paint from the sculptured figure on her tomb in Westminster Abbey with the aid of a penknife. One wonders what the reaction of the authorities would be today to such an event taking place in the Abbey.

In the preface to this volume the author states his intentions clearly, gives his general sources and his interpretation of them, and – way ahead of his time – points to the importance of dress in understanding the social and historical background of the period. This is a natural assumption in the modern teaching of history but was much less so in the compartmented approach of an earlier age.

The material for the second part of this work has been most carefully researched in the minutest detail. Medieval authorities have been studied, in particular Jean Froissart (c. 1337–1405), the French writer whose *Chronicles* give invaluable information about his time, notably concerning dress and the tradition of chivalry. Froissart was born in Valenciennes; in 1361 he came to England where Edward III appointed him chronicler of his court, and he subsequently travelled widely in England and elsewhere in Europe. His accounts of life in the fourteenth century are lively and interesting; but it needs to be borne in mind that his earlier descriptions were based extensively upon those of his predecessor Jean le Bel, and many of the later ones were derived from eyewitnesses other than himself.

There are also frequent references to the leading costume books produced in the eighteenth century, whose authors had attempted to break new ground in their time by providing a more accurate account than hitherto, based upon the antiquarian research available to them. Most notable of these were Dom Bernard de Montfaucon, whose *Monuments de la Monarchie françoise* was published in France in 1729–33, and the Englishman, Joseph Strutt, who published his impressive work about the people of England from Saxon times to his own day in 1775–6.

Detailed information is given about specific styles of dress in the Middle Ages, much of which is borne out in present-day study. Hamilton Smith tells us about tartan textile weaves in 'A Scots Knight' (page 131), when he is describing Scottish Highland dress. This particular type of chequer weave made from a striped warp and striped weft was not unique to Scotland or even to Britain, but fairly sophisticated versions were being woven there – as a cottage industry – from the later Middle Ages. The clan tartans, we now know, are of much more recent introduction and date from the later eighteenth century, well after the '45, when Bonnie Prince Charlie's army was defeated at Culloden. In the description of the courtiers of the time of Richard II (page 157), there is reference to piked shoes, that strange and inconvenient fashion of the late fourteenth century for extension to the footwear well beyond the actual toes of the foot. That this style existed is well documented, but the author repeats descriptions which considerably exaggerate the fashion.

The modern reader may find some of the nomenclature, as well as the spelling, unfamiliar, but it is always clear what is meant and the names of garments and styles given are not too different from the ones which we now adopt. In a few instances the author refers to a garment or decorative feature as being unfamiliar and he is unable to name it. One such example is mentioned in the description of William Beauchamp on page 159, where the 'belt hanging from the left shoulder' is a not uncommon fourteenth-century decorative addition which we should term a baldric; it was to be seen especially with this type of long gown– the houppelande.

The reader of today perusing this book cannot but evince admiration for the immense quantity of study which must have been incurred in years of preparation and collection of this material, admiration also for the careful evaluation of such material and honesty in admitting that some of the sources used might not prove to be entirely reliable. That the work is clearly an account written in a different age from our own is evident in a naïvety of acceptance of past data and in prejudice characteristic of the time – notably an English insularity in reference to Continental Europe – but these factors provide interest in such a historic manuscript. They are more than offset by appreciation of the detailed and vividly described text and the finely drawn and crafted colour plates. The source material of many of these plates, especially the later ones, is clearly recognizable. The colours are good and those inaccuracies which do occur are due largely to the methods of colour reproduction then available. The quality of printing and presentation is extremely high and this book will give pleasure and interest to many readers. It cannot fail to augment our stock of costume history works.

Doreen Yarwood

PREFACE

The Collection of Ancient Costumes exhibited in this Volume is selected from an immense mass of materials in the possession of the Author. It was originally begun for private amusement, and with a view to ascertain more correctly the Clothing, Arms, Decorations, and appearance of historic characters in the earliest periods of our annals, than had as yet been attempted. It was evident that, notwithstanding the labours of the accurate Mr. Strutt, truth of costume was little regarded either by Painters or Actors; and it seemed that this inattention to so essential a part of historic representation arose from a prejudiced idea in a great proportion of the Public, which conceived, that the pursuits of the Antiquary are dry, tasteless, and inelegant; and that to introduce upon the stage or upon the canvas material derived from such a source, must naturally destroy all beauty and harmony, and produce an insipid if not a burlesque effect. But an inspection of the following Specimens will tend to prove the notion groundless, and shew that when the outline of the human form is preserved tolerably correct, the draperies and armour will not be wanting in beauty or grandeur. Far from diminishing the impressions intended to be conveyed, an adherence to the Costume of the times represented will augment the illusion, and assist to explain the meaning.

The materials from which the Costumes are compiled, are Monumental Effigies, Brass Plates, Paintings on Glass, Seals, and ancient Illuminations. But as exact copies, or fac-simile representations, from subjects often mutilated, interest only the amateurs of Antiquities and perplex a young artist, it appeared to the Author an improvement to restore the mutilations, correct the drawing of the figures, and to vary and animate the attitudes of recumbent and kneeling effigies. But in venturing upon this deviation from rigid copy, he has been attentive to the time of his subject, and if a restoration is not the exact representative of what really occupied its place, it is at least taken from some contemporary subject, which from comparisons among a great multitude of materials, it was easy to select. For the colouring of such Monumental Statues or Seals, as were not indicated by armorial bearings or by the paintings of the originals, he has invariably had recourse to illuminations; and if statues have in general been preferred to drawings, it it because the sculptor was obliged to detail and render his subjects more intelligible than the painter. Between the endeavours of both it has been easy to imitate or to express their meaning; and it is hoped that the Costumes will present not only the true habits of the time, but also of the individuals portrayed.

A further inducement to take the subjects from Monuments, arose from their being (at least in several instances) Portraits which have not been engraved; and had the extent of the work admitted the propriety of carrying the idea further, the Author could have produced from his private collection a list of thirty Kings, many Queens, and a crowd of heroes. But the number of plates being limited, he trusts that the various specimens which are exhibited, will be sufficient to give a general view of the variations in the habits of our ancestors, and that it will be felt as a consequence, that historical representations on the theatre and on canvas are capable of being improved and heightened by a closer adherence to the habits of the times than has hitherto been practised.

In order to place the Collection in a proper order and fix a more limited idea of the periods when the different habits were in vogue, an attempt has been made to place, as near as possible, the true date of each Specimen. The Author has taken the year of the death of the personage represented, when the subject was taken from a Monument; that of the accession to a crown or title when it was copied from a Seal. Of Paintings on Glass and illuminated Manuscripts, the artist's time of life, a date in the book, the arms or badges of some distinguished person for whom it was made, and at length the comparison of several thousand sketches have served as criterions for their chronological classification; and by referring to the authorities under their proper heads, the true or approximate date will readily be found.

Some subjects are crowded together in a kind of historical composition, such as shipping, military engines, guns, tournaments and processions. Some of these are extracted from one MS. others from several, and consequently their dates are considerably more vague. Of the female habits, the limits of the work have not allowed room to exhibit a great variety, and their diversity is so extensive and the alterations of fashion so constant, that to have attempted a representation of a regular series would have been impossible, even if the Costumes had been carried through several volumes.

The lower orders of society have scarcely been noticed, because they excite less interest; and it may be considered as a general rule that the habits of those classes always imitate the fashions of their superiors, though at a humble distance, and deprived of those ornaments and superfluities which would encumber them in their avocations, or amount to a price above their means.

As the publication consists of selections from an extensive Collection, the arms under the figures do not shew the immediate connection which they have in the originals: but as this circumstances is not of much weight, they have therefore been introduced to embellish the work, and throw occasional light on the subjects.

It was the intention of the Author to have entered in his preface upon a general view of the ancient Costume, and in particular to have given more precise notions of the introduction, alterations, and improvements of ancient armour; but a sudden call to duties of a very different nature has compelled him, for the present, to relinquish his object, and to conclude the few remarks which he is now enabled to make, with the expression of his sincere acknowledgments for the favourable and indulgent reception which his work has obtained, and to apologize for the inaccuracies and *errata* which are to be found in it. This indulgence he trusts will be granted him, when his readers refer to the place from whence this preface is dated, and it is observed that he is not only cut off from all reference, but that his mind must necessarily be turned with attention towards the events which are passing around him.

His Majesty's Ship Horatio in the Room-pot
on the coast of Zeeland, 6th December, 1813.

COSTUME

OF THE ORIGINAL INHABITANTS OF THE

BRITISH ISLES

The investigation of savage life, and the various stages of improvement towards highly cultivated society, has been held, not only by the curious antiquary, but the discriminating philosopher, one of the most instructive as well as interesting subjects of human research. The avidity with which the accounts of newly discovered nations are read by the public has obtained for voyages and travels the character of the most fascinating species of narration; a fact which most fully demonstrates that an anxiety for acquaintance with our fellow creatures, whether we find them in the unexpanded bud of nature, or blooming forth in the richest colours and finest form of nurtured cultivation, is a principle deeply imbedded in our hearts.

Investigations of this kind, the arts and manufactures, the habits and customs, the religious and military characteristics, constitute the principal points of examination, and all these are intimately blended with COSTUME. In this point of view, the subject before us assumes its proper character, and rebuts the intemperate and hasty charge, of carrying with it the inferiority of not being worthy the consideration of a man of letters.[1]

ORIGINAL COSTUME OF THE BRITISH ISLES.

The Celtic tribes, in the progress of their migrations to the British isles, had, like the inhabitants of the South Sea, lost the antediluvian art of working metals,[2] and the fewer copper weapons which, from its extinction, glittered as rarities in the hands of their chiefs, disappeared, in all probability, ere they reached their ultimate destination. The Cimbrian savage therefore of Britain and Ireland, clad in the skin of the beast he had slain, issued in search of his prey from a cave hollowed by nature, or a hut scarcely artificial, which the interwoven twigs and leaves presented in a wood.[3] His weapons were a bow,[4] and some reed arrows, headed with flint, so shaped as to resemble the barbed metal piles of his ancestors, or pointed with bones sharpened to an acute edge. To assist in carrying these missile implements of carnage, he manufactured a quiver from the osier twigs that grew at hand. Or he proceeded to the chase, for his feats in hunting were but the peaceable representation of his deeds in war, with the spear and javelin, formed of long bones ground to a point, and inserted in an oaken shaft, held in the end of which by pegs, they became formidable weapons. Or he waged the savage fight with the death-dealing blows of the four-pointed oaken club. His domestic implements were a hatchet, sometimes used as a battle-axe, formed of an elliptical convexly-shaped stone, rounded by the current of a river, which he fastened to a handle with the fibres of plants; a large flint adze for felling timber, fitted for use in the same way, and a powerful stone hammer. To these he added a knife, formed also of a sharpened stone, which when used he held between his two first fingers and his thumb. Unbaked earthen vessels, the shells of fish, and a few wooden bowls, served to contain his meat and drink.[5] These were all his possessions, save his flocks and herds.

The partner of his life passed her time in basket-weaving,[6] or in sewing together with leathern thongs, or vegetable fibres, the skins of such animals as had fallen victims to her husband's prowess, employing for that purpose needles made of bone,[7] exactly similar to those used for the heads of arrows. Clad, by preference, in the skin, if to be procured, of the brindled ox, pinned together with thorns, ornamented with a necklace formed of jet or other beads, and with the wild flowers entwined within her long but twisted locks, she attractively became the soother of his toils.[8]

Such did the Cimbrian inhabitants of these isles appear to the wandering Phoenicians, and nearly such appeared the South Sea islanders to the celebrated Captain Cook.

[1]Dr. Meyrick, in three large quarto manuscript volumes, has collected, in the manner of Henry's History of Great Britain, whatever relates to the inhabitants of the Britannic Isles, from their first arrival till the termination in the year 703 of the British sovereignty in England; and it is from this elaborate work that the principal matter contained in the following pages has been extracted.

[2]The descendants of Cain had discovered the art of metallurgy. See Genesis.

[3]These are still remembered in the ancient British writings and traditions, where they are styled Cytiau Gwyddelod, *Woodlanders' huts*, and attributed to the aborigines, who are further said to have had foxes for their dogs, pole-cats for their domestic cats, and the like.

[4]The bwa or bow was an ancient Celtic weapon, known in this island before the Roman Arcus had made its appearance, though almost disused at the time of the arrival of the Romans. The estimation in which it was once held is evident from the following very ancient adage, "Nid hyder ond Bwa," "there is no reliance but on the bow."

[5]One of these was discovered in Dorsetshire, see Gough's Camden, vol.i.pl.ii.p.51. It was found in levelling a tumulus, called King Barrow, in the hamlet of Stowborough, 1767; and very neatly furrowed by lines hatched in different directions. Near it were also found in a large oak trunk a number of human bones, wrapt up in deer skins neatly sewed together, in a variety of small pieces, mixed with something like gold lace or wire.

[6]The ingenuity of the Britons (as is the case with the South Sea islanders) was much admired by the Romans, who, when they introduced into Italy the British Bascawd, adopted also its name, terming it Bascauda.

[7]Gwaëll signifies a needle, bodkin, skewer, or brooch, and it is curious that it is also the denomination of several bones; thus Gwaëll y goes, is the spindle bone of the leg, and Gwaëll yr ysgwydd, the shoulder-blade bone, which perhaps was split for needles or bodkins.

[8]It is not intended by these expressions to decide the question relative to the chastity of the British women. Their accusers are Cæsar, and Dion Cassius of Nieaea. The first of these says, "ten or twelve persons who are commonly near relations, as fathers, sons, and brothers, all have their wives in common; but the children are presumed to belong to that man to whom the mother was married." Dion, speaking of the people of Caledonia at the beginning of the third century, says, "they had all their wives in common, and brought up their children in common, not knowing to what father any of them belonged." This story might have been extracted from Cæsar, and applied to the Caledonians; for Chalcondyles, in the middle of the fifteenth century, speaking of Britain,

says that "the inhabitants welcome their guests with the embraces of their wives and daughters: and among friends they are lent and borrowed without shame." Dion likewise relates a story of the Empress Julia, wife of Severus: "As she one day rallied a British lady on the indecent custom of her country, the latter replied, 'Indeed we British women do herein much differ from the ladies of Rome, for we accompany the worthiest men, and do so openly, while here they are not ashamed to take any base fellow provided it be in secret.'" In opposition to this we have the testimony of that candid and authentic historian, Tacitus, who shews that Cartismandua brought herself into great disgrace for violating her marriage bed; and that the violence committed on the chastity of Boadicea's daughters was one principal cause of rebellion.

LIST OF THE PLATES

A Lady of the Reign of King Henry V.
Ralph Neville, 1st Earl of Westmore-
   land, &c.
Joan Pickering Lady Gascoigne.
Cecilia Lady Bryan Stapleton.
A Sportsman of rank, and a
   Gamekeeper.
Richard Beauchamp Earl of Warwick.
Joyce Lady Tiptoft.
Military Costumes of the Reign of
   King Henry VI.
King Henry VI. at his devotions.
Queen Margaret of Anjou.

Courtiers of the Reign of King Henry VI.
A Tournament, &c.
A Fisherman.
to 1500. Artillery, Warlike Machines,
   &c.
Pages and Valets.
A Warder or Porter.
Ships of the Reign of Edward IV.
English Archers.

THE TUDORS

A Lady and Gentleman.
Sir Rhys ab Thomas.

A BRITON OF THE INTERIOR.

The result of commerce is the progress of civilization. No sooner did the Phœnicians effect an amicable interchange with the natives of Britain and Ireland than they communicated to them[1] the art of manufacturing their warlike implements of metal. The composition was copper and tin, undoubtedly a soft or brittle substance, but evidenly superior to the bone and flint weapons of the rude natives, and of dazzling beauty in their eyes from its shining brightness. With so much policy did these foreign traders introduce this new semi-metal, that the method they took was sure to render it of universal demand. They at first exactly imitated the simple British weapons, and the spear and javelin-heads, as well as those for battle-axes, were made to be inserted in their respective handles. The figure represented in this plate, holds in his right hand a peculiar specimen of the Gwaew-fon or Fon-wayw, the blade of which was generally about a foot in length,[2] and nailed in a slit made in the ashen shaft, exactly in imitation of the rude native spear. The flat bladed javelin which the Phœnicians introduced was called Paled. But they did not rest contented with imitating the British and Irish weapons: having caused their manufactures to become greatly in demand, they introduced their own arms as patterns most worthy to be the esteemed models; and the shaft was soon fitted in the spear head, the handle in that of the battle-axe. The Briton here represented is clothed and armed as Cæsar represents the Cassii and other inhabitants of the internal parts of Britain to have been. Besides the Wayw-fon, he holds in his left hand the Tarian, or circular flat shield, rather more than two feet in diameter, with a hemispherical boss in the centre to admit his clenched fist. It was made of the same semi-metal, ornamented with concentric circles and intermediate knobs. Attached to a leathern thong is a large opening ring, on which is hung by a loop underneath its head the Bwyell-arv, Arv-vwyell, or Bwyell-ennilleg, the British battle-axe, greatly resembling an American tomahawk. He is clad in the skin of the brindled or spotted cow, called in his native tongue Brych, and by the Irish Breach. Instead of this some of the Britons wore the Ysgyn, which was the name for the skin of any wild beast, but more particularly the bear; while others assumed the Mantell, or sheep's skin cloak, according as they were herdsmen, hunters, or shepherds. In later times the Mantell, from being shorter, was worn only on horseback, and then termed Mantell werddonig, the Irish mantle, or Mantell gedenawg, the shaggy cloak.

Close by the side of this warrior appears his faithful dog, not only the trusty guardian of his hut, but his fierce and steady companion in war.

In the back-ground appears one of the Catterthuns, that termed the White in the shire of Angus in Scotland; so called from Cad yr ddîn, i.e. the fortress for time of war. The summit, however, of the mountain on which it stands is bifurced, with a fortress on each peak, the highest called the white, the other the black Catterthun. The White is a post of uncommon strength. It is of an oval form, and made of a stupendous dike of loose white stones, whose convexity from the base within to that without is 122 feet. On the outside of a hollow made by the disposition of the stones, a rampart surrounds the whole, round whose base is a

C.H.S. del.

Aquatinted by R.Havell.

A Briton of the Interior

deep ditch, and below that about a hundred yards, are vestiges of another that went round the hill. The area within the stony mound is flat. The greater extent of the oval is 436 feet, the transverse line 200. Near the east side is the foundation of a rectangular building, and on most parts are the foundations of others small and circular; all which once had their superstructures, the shelter of the possessors of the post. There is also a hollow now almost filled with stones, which was once the well of the place.[3]

The ancient Dîn or Dinas, and the Irish Dun, as the words import, were the alarm posts, in which the inhabitants of a district assembled in time of invasion, an event that rendered the construction of a proper and secure receptacle for that purpose absolutely requisite. Rowland[4] therefore does not hesitate to affirm, that from the people flocking to it, *dynesu* "to associate," occasioned the appellation Dinas, i.e. the place of association. But if this derivation, ultimately from *Dyn*, "a man or woman," be liable to objection, it may be observed that *Din* itself signifies "what surrounds" i.e. an entrenchment. From this name of the British citadels we have the Roman Dinum, Dinium, and Dunum; and also the Tune, Don, Ton, and Town of the Saxons. Dun is the same word in the Belgic dialect, whence it was principally used in England and Ireland. In this species of fortification the ancient Britons and Irish lodged their wives and children, and into it drove their cattle from the low adjacent country on any sudden invasion. Here they formed garrisons and made their stand, and from hence they sallied forth with confidence to repel the foe. Such fortresses were generally constructed on the most lofty hills, which, though from want of water they would be rendered untenable for any great length of time, were from the same cause subject to much wet; and thence enabled the warriors for a certain period to defend themselves. The Dinas therefore of necessity was the strongest kind of fortification, and we consequently always meet with it strengthened by several ramparts, as a fixed place of security in case of danger.

The Vignette at the bottom of the plate exhibits a battle-axe head and ring of the same kind of semi-metal, found at Tadcaster in Yorkshire, which further authorises the idea that these axes were worn suspended from the shoulder.

[1] That the art was communicated to the Britons is clear from the discovery of moulds for spear, arrow, and axe heads in Britain and Ireland.

[2] The specimen here given differs somewhat from the generality of the blades of the Gwaew-fon, being near three inches broad where it is inserted in the shaft, and suddenly becoming and continuing only one inch in breadth, while in its broken state it is fourteen inches long. The Irish name for these spears was Laineach-catha or war-spears. See one found in Britain in Co.Merioneth.

[3] King's Munimenta Antiqua, vol. I. p. 27.

[4] Mona Antiqua.

A BELGIC BRITON, AND ONE OF THE CASSITERIDES.

The arts of dressing wool and flax, and of spinning them into cloth, are too complicated to render it probable that they were equally invented in many different countries, like the more simple arts, but rather that they were communicated by one people to another. We may therefore presume, that to the Phœnicians the inhabitants of these isles were indebted not only for highly improved implements of war, but for the first hints towards the manufacture of cloth. Yet the advantages which the Britons might have been expected to receive in this most useful art, were but local: for except the inhabitants of Cornwall and the Scilly isles, with whom the Phœnicians more immediately traded, we do not find any rapid improvement in the cloathing of the other parts of the country. But this was not the case with the Irish; they had long been acquainted with the art, and probably the Tinea Scuit, (Celto-Scythian race) generally denominated the Milesian Colony, brought it with them from Spain. Thus the names of the materials, machinery, & c. are similar in the Irish, the Chaldee, the Hebrew, and the Arabic languages, nor have the descendants of this people at the present day lost the celebrity their ancestors had acquired for the manufacture.

With respect to Britain it is most probable, that to Gaul it was indebted for the first permanent instructions in these most valuable arts, and we may therefore conclude that the inhabitants of the southern maritime parts of the country were well acquainted with dressing, spinning, and weaving both flax and wool, and that they practised these arts much in the same manner as the people of Gaul.

Of the several kinds of cloth made in Gaul, one, according to Strabo, was made of a coarse harsh kind of wool, which being woven very thick, was rendered extremely warm, and consequently was the fabric of which the winter cloaks were manufactured. Another kind was made of fine wool, and dyed several different colours;[1] and being spun into yarn was woven chequerwise, which made it form small squares, some of one colour, and some of another. In this we may not improperly contemplate the tartan of the Highlands, and of this the Gauls and Britons made their summer garments.[2] The Gauls manufactured also a kind of cloth or felt of wool without either spinning or weaving; and of the wool which was shorn from this in dressing it they made their mattresses. The Britons seem to have done the same, and hence the denomination Bryean, which became the universal name for woollen cloths, being derived from *Brwg*, "brush-wood," owing to its similarity in appearance. This cloth or felt is said to have been so strong and firm when vinegar was used in making it, that it would resist the blow of a sword, and was even considered as some defence against fire.[3]

We have direct evidence that the Gauls and Britons excelled in the art of dying cloth, and possessed some valuable secrets in it unknown to other nations. Pliny enumerates several herbs used for this purpose, and tells us that these people dyed purple, scarlet, and other colours from them alone. The peasantry in Wales have the knowledge of several indigenous plants, valuable for imparting colours, and use the leaves of the foxglove and sorrel as preparatives for the purpose. They

[15]

extract a beautiful yellow from tansy, brown from nut leaves, and other colours from lichens. But the herb which the Britons chiefly used for this purpose was the *glastrum* or woad, called in the native language Y glâs, Glaslys, and Glaiarllys, from Glâs, blue; and they seem to have been led to the discovery of its valuable properties in dying cloth, from the former use of it in tatooing their bodies. The sky-blue long continued to be the favourite colour of the ancient Britons, and particularly of the Caledonians, and still holds a pre-eminence in Wales, although red is much esteemed.

In the last plate we had a Briton represented clad in a skin, and took occasion to notice the Ysgin, Brych, and Mantell. We have now to observe, that as these garments must during the summer, when not used, have been frequently destroyed, or at least disfigured by insects, the next improvement would be to separate the fleece from the skin, and the hair from the hide, and manufacturing vestments of the latter only. The new garment thus obtained was called Rhuchen, i.e. a cloak of skin or leather; and although some advantage in durability was obtained, yet the coldness of the material must have considerably detracted from the value of the article itself. The wool and the hair were next therefore viewed as likely, if manufactured, to form a more warm and agreeable species of clothing.

Though the hair and wool of animals were probably the first, they were not long the only materials that were used in making cloth for garments. The attention and industry of mankind soon discovered several other things fit for answering that purpose, particularly the long, slender, and flexible filaments of flax and hemp. The manufacturing of cloths of the inner rind of trees split into long threads, which was practised by the Britons as well as the modern inhabitants of the South Sea isles, probably led to the use of these vegetables substances, if the art was not indeed acquired from the Gauls. That the Irish were early skilled in this manufacture, we learn from the peculiar terms in their language expressive of its various concomitants and we learn from Pliny that the art of making this beautiful kind of cloth prevailed not only over all Italy, but also in Spain, Gaul, Germany, and Britain. They also knew the art of washing and bleaching linen; and the same author tells us they put certain herbs, particularly the roots of wild poppies into the water to make it more efficacious in bleaching. For the purposes of washing, they made soap of the fat of animals, and the ashes of vegetables (the modern pot-ash), the invention of which this author attributes to the Gauls.[4]

The yarn, as before observed, having been dyed in imitation of the brindled oxen's skin, the cloth manufactured from it in stripes and chequers was called Breach as well as Brycan by the ancient Britons, and Breacan by the Irish, whence the Braccae of the Roman writers. The utility of this manufacture, and the dazzling effects of a variety of colours, rendered it so much esteemed by the chieftains, that it was not long confined to one garment.

Before the Romans entered Britain the habits of its chiefs consisted of a *Pais*, or close coat or covering for the body, deriving that name from *Py*, inward, and *Ais*, the ribs; and which, under the denomination of Cota,[5] formed a part of the Irish dress. This is what Dio calls χιλΩν, a tunic, and describes it as being παμποικιλος, of various colours, and χρωμασι πανλσδαπσις δινηθισμενσς, chequered with various colours in divisions. It was open before

A Belgic Briton and  *one of the Cassiterides*

like a shirt in order to enable the wearer to put it on, and had sleeves which were close, yet long, and reaching to the wrist; and extended itself to the middle. Below this began the *Llawdyr*, or loose pantaloons, which wrapped closely round the thighs and legs, terminating at the ankles.[6] These were also plaided, and called by the Irish Brigis, and by the Romans Brages and Braccae, whence the word Breeches.[7] Over the Pais was thrown the mantle or cloak, called by the Romans *Sagum*, from the Celtic word Saic, which, according to Varro, signified a skin or hide, and the truth of his testimony is borne out by the Irish Seiche.

On the feet were either the *Esgidiau*, shoes, so called from Es-cîd, protection from hurt, similar to the Brog of the Irish, which were made of raw cow-hide that had the hair turned outwards, and coming up to the ankles; or the *Bwtais* or Butis, the more modern Buskin.[8]

On his head was placed the Irish *Capa* or Caba, the British Cappan, i.e. cap, which derived its name alike from the Irish Caban, a cabin, and the British Cab, the hut, which was made in the form of a cone, with wattles stuck in the ground, and fastened together at top; a shape preferred by the Egyptians, and adopted by many nations. It is somewhat singular that the form of this ancient pointed cap is to this day exhibited in what the children of the Welsh peasantry call Cappan cyrnicyll, the horn-like, or cornute cap, made of rushes tied at top, and twisted into a band at bottom, exactly in the form of a cone, and like the ancient cabins. The form of this ancient cap was long retained by the Irish under the denomination Biorraid, and was the prototype of their helmets,[9] but the Britons seem to have made an improvement in it, by lowering the top, and making a projecting poke over the forehead to protect the eyes, and this they termed *Penguwch*. In process of time, however, the *Penguwch* seems to have been discarded by the men, and worn solely by the women, as in a MS. entitled Hên ddevodau, or old customs, the following passage occurs, "A yellow Penguwch used to be worn by a woman newly married." The men next adopted the *Hatyr*, Ata, or Hat, of which many with convex crowns appear on the British coins, and a Gaulish female with a flattened one is given by Montfaucon, in his Antiquités expliquées par Figures," &c.

This kind of dress was however worn only by the chieftains of the British isles, and ladies of rank: their dependants were still clothed in skins or leather.

Diodorus Siculus thus describes the habit of the Belgic Gauls, "They wore tunics, (the Pais or Cota) flowered in various compartments, and of different colours; close trowsers (the Llawdyr or Brigis) which they called Bracae. Moreover, they wore Sagae manufactured of striped cloth, thicker for winter, and thinner in summer, fastening them with laces, so as to resemble several flowers, and set very thick. The arms that they use are shields covering almost the whole of a man, and varied only by some private insignia thereupon; some wearing the representation of beasts in brass, fashioned as well for defence as ornament. They moreover fortify their heads with scull-caps of brass from which there issue great appendages, made prolix for the sake of ostentation. Some of these have horns of the same substance, or the representations of birds or quadrupeds expressed on them. They use barbaric straight trumpets, of a kind peculiar to themselves, which when inflated yield a horrid echo, and instil the terrors of war into those who are thus called together on emergences. They wear also breast-plates made of iron work. Others, content with the gifts of nature, fight naked. Instead of small swords, they carry long two-handed swords (Spathæ), which are suspended across their right thighs by iron or brass chains. Some girt their tunics with belts adorned with gold or silver. They moreover carry, for throwing, lances which they term Lankia (called in the Irish language, which is closely allied to the Belgic, Laincach), the iron blade of which equals a cubit in length, while the shaft is not much longer, and its breadth not wanting much of two palms. The swords of some are not less than the javelins (or Saunia) of others, except that the blades of the javelins are broader than those of the swords. Some of these are of a straight form, others curved, so as to bend through their whole length, by which they not only cut in the blow, but even tear the flesh, and when withdrawn from the wound dreadfully lacerate the excoriation."

Speaking of the gold produced in Gaul, he further says:– "In this manner an immense quantity of gold is collected, which not only the women, but even the men, apply to the purposes of ornament. They wear armillae fastened round their wrists, as well as bracelets on their arms, massive torques of pure unadulterated gold round their necks, rings worthy of mention on their fingers, and above all, golden breast plates."

The first circumstance to notice here is the casque with brazen horns and large appendages. Though none of these have ever been discovered in Britain or Ireland, and we are told by Herodian and Xiphilin that the Britons were without them, yet the coins ascribed to Cunobelin exhibit a scull-cap ornamented round the rim, and one with the prolix appendages.[10] The next thing worthy of notice is the straight barbaric trumpet. One of these, six feet four inches long, and three inches and a half at its lower extremity, was dug up from a turbary on the lands of Becan in the county of Mayo in Ireland, in August 1791, being found nine feet below the surface. It was of willow, and made of two pieces fastened together by a spiral band of brass. Such are called in the old Irish tales Buadh-vail, or "victory's mouth-piece," and said to have been military instruments of music, used only on emergencies, and capable of producing so tremendous a sound, that it might be heard at the distance of seven miles.[11] The Spathæ, or two-handed swords, were used by both the Britons and Irish, the former of whom termed them Cleddyv-hîr deuddwrn, i.e. long two-handed swords, which are said to have been without points, and therefore the ensis sine mucrone of Tacitus,[12] and the latter, Dolaimghen, or pointless two-handed swords. With respect to the Laineach, or Lagean, evidently the Lankia, the following anecdote from that very ancient Irish Cronicle the Laebha Gabala is a most striking confirmation. Labra Lonseach, *after his return* from exile *in Gaul*, about two centuries and a half before Christ, brought the Lagean, a sort of broad-edged lance into use; whence the people of Leinster are said to have acquired the name of Lagenians, and their country that of Coigea-Lagean.[13] But the description given by Diodorus is very close to the account we have of the British Llavnawr or blade-weapon, which is said to have been seven feet long, four only of which was the shaft.[14] The Saunia was probably also the name of a javelin used by the ancient Irish, for we have still in that language Sonnaim, to pierce through.[15] The straight swords of the Irish were

[19]

called Cliabh, and Claidheamh dorn chrann,[16] and the curved ones Airben, from Airbe, a rib.[17] Armillæ and bracelets were worn by the Irish and Southern Britons and torques of gold, silver, and iron have been dug up both in Britain and Ireland.[18] Golden rings are found in the tumuli of both countries, and Druidical breast-plates of gold, to which class they were probably confined, have likewise been discovered in Ireland.

Upon the whole then, having thus put Diodorus to the test, we have ample materials for the Costume of the Belgic tribes of Britain. The right-hand figure therefore in the plate represents a British warrior of the southern parts of England. He wears a Pais or tunic ornamented with an embroidered border. It is coloured a brownish yellow, because that was a favourite dye of the Gauls and other Celtic nations.[19] Over the shoulders is thrown the Saic or Sagum of checquer work, in which the predominant colour was commonly red. His legs and thighs are covered with the Llawdyr or Braccae, and he wears shoes of untanned leather. On his arms are bracelets, round his neck a massive torque,[20] and about his waist a belt to which by a brazen chain is suspended his brazen sword.[21] In his right hand he holds the hunting spear, the Laineach Sealgach of the Irish, and Gwaëw-Hela of the Britons,[22] and on his head he wears the Cappan Cyrnicyll, or cornuted cap. The inhabitants of Cornwall and the Scilly isles, however, were of a more peaceable character, and from their intercourse with foreign merchants, more civilized and hospitable.[23] According to Strabo they were habited in long black garments like tunics, wearing their mustachios hanging down upon their breasts like wings. They were a quiet, inoffensive people, and when walking abroad, they held large staves in their hands, which made them resemble furies in a tragedy.[24] The left-hand figure in this plate exhibits one of these people, and is principally remarkable for his hair, which greatly resembles the Gaulish fashion, according to Diodorus Siculus. Of these he says, "They frequently wash their hair with a lixivium made from chalk, turning it back from the forehead over the crown of the head, and letting it fall down their necks. This gives them the appearance of Satyrs and Pans. They indeed allow it to grow so thick that it scarce differs from a horse's mane. Some shave their beards, others make them grow in a modish way. The nobility (i.e. chieftains) are shaved, but wear mustachios, which hang down so as to cover their mouths, so that when they eat and drink, they brush their victuals or dip into their liquids."[25] In this Costume we may contemplate the British merchant.

The back-ground presents a view of a circular entrenchment, called Caer Morus, in the parish of Cellan and county of Cardigan. The Caer, in contradistinction to the Dinas, seems to have been the name applied to such entrenchments as were thrown up on the march or retreat of an army, where time would not permit a fortifaction of more studied and laborious construction. We therefore generally find the Caer consist of one single vallum and ditch. From the resemblance of the Roman Castra to these, the Britons termed those entrench-ments by the same name; Caer is itself derived from Cae, a word equally used in the British and Irish languages to denote an enclosure; and all places called Caer by the Britons, were by the Saxons denominated Ceaster, Cester, Cister, and Chester. Similar in a great measure to the Caer was the Irish Rath, which has been falsely attributed to the Danes, since there is positive proof in the accounts of the life of St. Patrick, that they existed some centuries before.[26]

The vignette at the bottom of the plate represents the Covinus, or single horse war chariot, with flat circular wooden wheels. The body is represented of wicker, as that kind of material was used in other defences by the Britons. The driver is standing on the shaft, and leaning against the horse.[27] The shafts for this carriage were armed with hooks, and its axles with a small kind of scythe blade,[28] for tearing and cutting all who were so unfortunate as to come within its reach. The British name for this is now lost, but its derivative may be traced in the expression cywain yd "to carry corn." Ancient authors describe it as made very slight, capable of containing only one man besides the charioteer.[29]

[1]Plin. Hist. Nat. lib. viii. c. 48. and Diod. Sicul. lib. v. It was sometimes worked in stripes, and sometimes in chequers; examples of both are to be seen at this day in the gowns, petticoats, and aprons of the Welsh peasantry, and more particularly of the latter in the Highland plaids. It is a singular fact, that in the South Sea cloths, manufactured from the bark of trees, we have not only the stripes and chequers, but the very identical patterns of the Welsh: doubtless, therefore, they must have been those of the ancient Britons.

[2]Dion. Cassins calls Boadicca's garment παμποικιλον

[3]Plin. Hist. Nat. lib. viii. c. 48.

[4]Probably they employed at first the ashes of the fern on which they roasted their venison. Fern ashes are used at this day by the peasantry in Wales for the same purpose.

[5]That is a close covering, whence the verb Cotaigham. It need scarcely be observed, that from this garment and its name, we derive the modern Coat.

[6]Martial, lib. xi. Epig. 21. Diodorus and Strabo.

[7]The Irish likewise call the trowser Triubhas.

[8]Ware's Hist. of Ireland, edit. Harris, p. 178. Birt's Letters from the Highlands, vol. ii. p. 115, 185, and 186; and Giraldus Cambrensis. The shoes of the Gauls, according to Montfaucon, had two slits down the front; whereas, the Saxons' shoes had only one: but shoes have been dug up in England made of one piece of untanned leather, slit in several places, in each of which holes were made, through which a thong passed, which being drawn tight, fastened them round the foot like a purse. See Phil. Trans.

[9]See the representation of Mac Murrogh king of Leinster in Smith's Ancient Costume of England; and also that of a Scots knight in the same: see also the plates to Ledwich's Antiquities of Ireland, by which it appears to have been worn so late as the time of James I.

[10]See Whitaker's History of Manchester, vol. I. p. 244, 8vo.edit. See also Gough's Camden. The Gaulish coins given by Montfaucon afford some specimens of the horned helmet. The confused account of an Irish peasant finding a scull-cap is too vague to be relied on.

[11]See Royal Irish Academy's Transactions, vol. IV. p. 33, for a more detailed account. See also the Vignette title-page of this work.

[12]Vit. Agric. C. 36. See also Herodian, lib.iii.c. 46, and Horsley's Brit. Rom. p. 195.

[13]See O'Flaherty's Ogygia Domest. p. 269.

[14]One of these found in Cardiganshire is described in the Gentleman's Magazine. Several have been dug up in Ireland, and representations given in the Collectanea de Reb. Hib. and Gough's edition of Camden's Britannia. See Viguette to plate ix.

[15]Shaw's Gaelic Dictionary, sub voce.

[16]See one of the former in the Arch. vol. III. pl. xix. the latter were swords with fist guards, since retained by the Highlanders.

[17]One of these appears in the hand of a Northern Briton on horseback, sculptured on a stone in Horseley's Britannia Romana.

[18]Two of gold, weighing 25 oz. and five feet in length, have been lately discovered in the county of Meath.

[19]Of this the Emperor Tetricus gave an instance when he appeared in the habit of a Belgic Gaul. See the Triumph of Aurelian as described by Vopiscus. Camden, in his Anuales Elizabethæ, mentions the Irish chieftain O'Neil and his followers to have visited the Queen of England in saffron-coloured tunics. These, however, were not dyed in saffron, but by a kind of lichen that grows on the rocks, and is still prepared by the Irish as Archill. It gives that shade of yellow that borders on a dark brown. This lichen is also used in Wales for the same purpose, its name being Cwppa-Cerrig, i.e. rock-cups.

[20]It is copied from that found on Quantock Hill, being of twisted gold. See Arch. vol. xiv. pl. xxiii. Two specimens of the torque have been lately found in the county of Meath; but being of wreathed bars nearly five feet in length, were probably for the waist: each bar consists of four flat bands, most accurately united along one of their edges, and spirally twisted throughout. The extremities are smooth, solid, truncated cones. suddenly reflected backwards, so as to form hooks which mutually clasp each other. Perpendicularly from the base of one of these cones proceeds a gold wire a quarter of an inch thick, and eight inches long, terminating also in a solid knob: this last appendage is deficient in every other torque hitherto discovered: the weight of the whole torque is 25 oz. The Egyptians, Persians, and even the Greeks and Romans, are said to have adorned themselves with torques in the early periods of their history, and they continued in Wales to a very later period. The torque was at first confined to the royal and sacerdotal characters, but afterwards extended to the military. Scheffer bestows eight chapters on the torques in his very learned and ingenious treatise "De Antiquorum Torquibus Syntagma." He maintains that three species of ornaments were included under the generic name Torque, viz. 1. The Torques proper, called Carella cum fibulis, composed of rings and hooks linked together like a chain. 2. The Circulus, formed of rods of gold laid together like cords, and twisted into a wreath: and 3. the Monile, a plain broad collar of gold, which fitted close to the neck.

[21]This is copied from one found in Ireland two feet three inches long. See Arch. vol. III. pl. xix.

[22]See Collect. de Reb. Hib. pl. xi. fig. 5, and Arch. vol. xvi. pl. I. These have two loops or hollows on each side, and are so represented in the plate here given, though these appendages are not confined to the hunting spears. Sometimes instead of these loops two apertures appear in the blade, and this probably belonged to the Slidh cheam-rainhar chro-fhairsing catha, heavy headed, broad-eyed spear of battle.

[23]Diodorus Siculus, lib. v.

[24]Strabo, lib. iii.

[25]Diod. Sicul. lib. v.

[26]See Gough's Camden, vol. III. p. 482. The Castell of the Britons was a name derived from the Roman Castellum, and consequently of later date.

[27]This is taken from an Irish car in Bushe's Hibernia curiosa, compared with a drawing by Mr. Oben. Many such are still used in Glamorganshire. See King's Munim. Antiq. vol.I. p.107, and the plate p. 112.

[28]See one of these, thirteen inches long, in the Collect. de Reb. Hib. vol. iv. pl. xi. Thus Silius Italicus, "Agmina falcifero circumvenit arcta Covino."

[29]Mela, lib. iii. c. 6.; and Tacit. Vit. Ag. c. 36.

A MAÆATA AND CALEDONIAN.

Ⅱ nations that wear but little clothes shew their ostentation by having the various exposed parts of their bodies highly tatooed. Pomponius Mela, who flourished about the year of our Lord 45, tells us, accordingly, that the "Britons dyed their bodies with woad, but whether for ornament, or any other reason, is not known." The Maæatæ and Caledonians, i.e. inhabitants of the plains and forests in North Britain, had not at this time been discovered to the Romans; and even when they were by Julius Agricola, all that we hear concerning them is that they were in a state of barbarity.[1] So late as the time of the emperor Severus they are represented as almost naked, wearing about their necks and bellies torques covered with twisted iron wire;[2] which they regarded as great ornaments, and prized as highly as the other tribes did theirs of silver and gold. Yet it would seem that this nakedness did not proceed from want of garments, which were probably laid aside for the fight,[3] but from pride, for they painted their bodies with various colours, and having punctured the skin, rubbed into the incisions, which represented different animals, &c. the juice of the woad. They either knew not the use of shoes or did not care to wear them.[4] Isidorus describes the method of tatooing in these words: "They squeeze the juice of certain herbs into figures made on their bodies with the points of needles." And Solinus says, as this operation was performed with sharp needles it was very painful; and (as in the South Seas at this day) those were esteemed the bravest men, who bore it with the greatest fortitude, and received the deepest punctures to imbibe the greatest quantities of paint.

The right-hand figure in this plate represents one of the Catini, or people who used the Cat, a club with four spikes, which he is enabled to dart forward and recover again by means of the thong attached.[5] These Britons dwelt along the sea-shore of Strathnavern, and their weapon, though a simple one, was formidable. The left-hand figure represents a Caledonian with his spear in his hand,[6] made to fight with either in close combat, or to use as a missile weapon, having a thong affixed for its recovery when darted. This was called Aseth, and was probably of ash, as thence arose the proverb Aseth ni flyco nid da, "the Aseth that will not bend is not good." At the butt end of it is a round ball of brass filled with pieces of metal, to make a noise when engaged with cavalry.[7] This ball in the Highland-Scotch or Irish language was called Cnopstara, i.e. the active ball.[8] Both are ornamented with torques and chains, and armed with swords.

The back-ground represents the Lan-y-on Cromlêch in Cornwall, the covering stone of which is 19 feet long, and 47 feet in girt; and is placed so high that a man on horseback may ride under it. Lan-y-on signifies the enclosure of On, the Arkite divinity,[9] and therefore exactly implies what all Cromlêchs were intended to be, representations of the Noachic Ark.[10] *Crom*, both in Welsh and Irish, signifies a bending in or concavity,[11] and Llêch or Leach, a stone. In composition the words in the Irish language denote "the stone of punishment or degradation, and the bed of death,"[12] all having a reference to Noah's enclosure in the Ark. It is also called in Welsh, Llôg, the stone of the Ark,[13] and by Aneurin the Bard, Llogell Byd, the Ark of the world, words of the same reference as the Irish name. But in the Triads this circumstance is more particularized; for it is in them termed the prison of Ooeth and Anoeth, "wrath" and "the remission of wrath," as commemorative of the anger of the Almighty when he destroyed the nations from the face of the earth, and of his goodness again by the repeopling the world from the family saved in the ark. When the Arkite religion became blended with Sabian idolatry, the cromlêch was placed in the Cylch cynghrair, or circle of federation, and called Llêch o chymmraint, the flat-stone of social privilege, and Crair Gorsedd, the token of the bardic convention. In it were performed various ceremonies relating to the bardic orders, with a reference to the great event of the Deluge, and the primary one of these was the sheathing of a sword, as a token of their being devoted to *peace, and insulated from all the parties and disputes of the world*. Being peculiarly dedicated to the Arkite genius it was entitled Maen Cetti, the stone of Cetti or the Ark, and the raising of it was, according to the Triads, one of the three mighty labours of the isle of Britain. In it were celebrated all the mysteries of Ceridwen or Cetti, and in it her mystical cauldron was said to be warmed by the breath of nine damsels.[14] Here the adventurous aspirant beheld some of the mysteries of Druidism, when admitted behind the veil, on which was pourtrayed the effigies of the goddess, and which on such occasions was hung over its entrance.[15]

At a distance behind this is a mountain east of Cellan in Cardiganshire, on each extremity of which is a Carn.[16] The Carn or Cairn is a heap of stones thrown over the urns in which were deposited the ashes of the dead. These were placed in a cistvaen or stone chest within, called also by the Welsh Gwely, a bed, and by the Irish Leaba, a word of the same import, or Colla, a sleeping place. As such kind of monuments contained no inscription to declare to posterity the name and actions of the deceased, short accounts of them were formed into triplets, and under the title of "the graves of the warriors," handed down by oral tradition.[17]

Below the plate is an example of the Logan or Rocking Stone,[18] near Drew Steignton in Devonshire, which is ten feet high, easily rocked, of granite, and seated in the channel of a river.[19] These prodigious stones the Druids had the art to persuade their infatuated votaries were inspired with the spirit of the in-dwelling deity, and to this awful test they brought the supposed criminal over whose head the sword of justice was suspended, and the descent of which was alone delayed, till the animated mass, as he approached to touch it, by its tremulous motion declared him guilty.

[1]Tacit. in Vit. Ag.

[2]One of these is represented in the Archaeologia, vol. XIV. pl. xix.

[3]This was practised by the Highlanders at the battle of Killicranky.

[4]Horodian in Vit. Sever. lib. iii. c. 46. Xiphilin ex Dione Nic. in Sever.

[5]See Camb. Register, vol. II.

[6]This spear head is taken from one engraved in the Philosophical Transactions for 1796, part 2; and is of the

A Maxata and Caledonian.

broad leaf kind. It was a favourite shape with the Britons, and many spear heads preserve the form, varying only in breadth. See Arch. vol. XVI. pl. liv. and others.

[7]Xiphilin ex Dione Nicæo in Sever.

[8]Dr. Macpherson's Crit. Diss. p. 144. He says the spear itself was denominated Triniframma. The ball seems the prototype of the bells for waggon horses.

[9]See Bryant's Analysis of Mythology; also his Plagues of Egypt: and Taliesin's Cadeir teyrn On, or the Chair of the sovereign On. In another poem he identifies this divinity with the On of Heliopolis.

[10]Davies's Mythology of the Druids.

[11]Hence in Irish it is also used to denote a reverential bending of the body.

[12]Archæologia, vol. XVI. p. 265.

[13]Owen's Welsh Diet.

[14]See the Poem of Taliesin on the Spoils of the Deep.

[15]Davies's Mythology of the Druids.

[16]Wales is so abundant in these sepulchres that Taliesin calls it Cymry carneddawg.

[17]See two specimens of collections of these in the Archaiology of Wales, vol. I. The subject of ancient British and Irish burial and funeral rites is of too extensive a nature to be introduced here. In Dr. Meyrick's MS. before noticed it occupies nearly forty quarto pages. The grave of Vortigern in the mountains of Rhuvoniawg, and that of Hengist at Coningsborough, had their contents been properly attended to, would have afforded us certain specimens of the tumulus interment in the fifth century.

[18]Llogan seems to have a connection with Llôg, the stone of the covenant, and the stone of the Ark: Col Vallencey thinks *Rocking* is a corruption of Ruachan, i.e. divining or angury.

[19]See Polwhele's History of Devonshire, and Borlase's Antiq. of Cornwall.

A MOUNTED BRITISH WARRIOR.

All the British and Irish youths, the Bardic order excepted, were trained to the use of arms from their infancy, continued in them to their old age, and were always ready to appear when called by their leaders into actual service.[1] Their very diversions and amusements were of a martial and manly cast, greatly contributing to encrease their agility, strength, and courage.[2] Their kings and chieftains were consequently surrounded with a chosen band of brave and noble youths, who passed their time in hunting and martial sports, and were ready at a moment's warning to embark with the eagerness of American Indians in any military expedition.[3]

The armies of the Britannic isles were not divided into distinct corps, with officers of different ranks, as in the Roman legions, and the regiments of modern days, but all the warriors of each particular clan or tribe formed a distinct band, commanded by its pencenedyl. This disposition had its advantages and defects; for while each respectively was strengthened by the ties of blood as well as honour, so many equal independent societies were liable to be affected by intrigue, and feel the effect of mutual jealousy. But the tribes were generally faithful to their respective chiefs,[4] as the hitherto strong attachment of the Highland clans to their lairds is an existing proof. Thus the British Triads hold out as examples "the three faithful tribes,"[5] and condemn to infamy "the three treacherous tribes." The troops which composed the armies of the ancient Britons and Irish were of three kinds, infantry, cavalry, and those who fought from chariots. Of these the infantry was by far the most numerous body, and composed the strength of their armies;[6] while the charioteers were the most formidable and distinguished.[7] The cavalry were mounted on small but hardy mettlesome horses, which they managed with great dexterity. They rode without saddles,[8] and the bits of their bridles were of bone.[9] They were armed with clubs, wooden slings,[10] small curved swords, or long spears with shields.[11] The figure exhibited in this plate is formed from the designs on three British coins.[12] He has on his head the brazen helmet, with its huge appendages mentioned by Diodorus the Sicilian, wears the Mantell gedenawg, or shaggy cloak, appointed for horsemen in the Welsh laws, the trowsers, and shoes, and bears in his hand a ponderous club.

It was usual for the horsemen of the Britannic isles, as well as those of the Gauls and Germans, to dismount when occasion required and fight on foot, having their horses so well trained, that they stood quietly where they were left till their masters returned.[13] It was also a common practice to mix an equal number of foot soldiers who were famed for swiftness with the cavalry, each of whom held by a horse's mane, and kept pace with him in all his motions.[14] This mode of fighting was practised by the Highlanders of the Scots' army so late as the civil wars in the time of King Charles I.[15]

[1]Tacit. Vit. Ag. c. 29, Cæs. de Bel. Gall. lib. vi. c. 14.

[2]Part of the martial sports, particularly those for cavalry, are still practised at the Welsh weddings.

[3]Tacitus relates the same of the Germans. Hence the fondness of the Britons for such names as Cadvan, conspicuous in battle; Cadwaladyr, supreme leader of battle, &c; and of the Irish for those of Boiromh, the divine warrior, or god of war, and such like.

[4]See Cæsar's account of Divitiacus in Bel. Gall.

[5]Three tribes are also celebrated for putting the fetters or bands of their horses on their own feet, so as to engage coupled; a circumstance also recorded of the Cimbri, who fought against the Romans, B.C. 109.

[6]Tacit. Vit. Agrie. c. 12.

[7]Cæs. Bel. Gall.

[8]Observing these with the Romans they called them Cyvrwy, i.e. an accompanying superfluity.

[9]Strabo.

[10]The coins which appear to exhibit slings are one in Gibson's Camden, coin 19th; Speed, p. 173 and 186; and Whitaker, vol. I. p. 305.

[11]A naked Briton on horseback, with the Airben or curved sword, appears on a carved altar found in Northumberland. A Briton on horseback, with a spear, is given in Whitaker's Manchester, vol. II. p. 7. See also those in Gibson's Camden, and Henry's Hist. of Britain. On one of these coins is a horse without a rider, bearing something like a shield of the lozenge shape.

[12]Two in Whitaker's Manchester, vol. II. p. 7, on which are legends in the ancient British character, and one in Gough's Camden, vol. I. coin the 26th. This last gives the authority for the club. See also Gough, coin 36; Whitaker, vol. I. p. 305, the four coins, and p. 344, the third coin, for the helmets and mantles.

[13]Cæs. Bel. Gall. l. iv. c. 2.

[14]Ibid. l. i. c. 2.

[15]Memoirs of a Cavalier, p. 142.

C.H.S. del.

Aquatinted by R. Havell.

A Mounted *British Warrior.*

BRITISH FISHING AND HUSBANDRY.

From the warlike we turn with pleasure to the peaceful occupations of the ancient Britons and Irish. The plate before us represents two fishermen; one in his coracle, holding in one hand his paddle, and the other his net; and one carrying his coracle on his back, held thereon by a twisted wicker cord passing from the seat round his forehead, and by the paddle being placed transversely. This he is about to launch and assist his fellow fisherman by managing the other end of the net.

As the Britons from their first arrival in this island continued to pass and repass to Gaul, and sometimes to navigate the German Ocean; and as the Irish not only traded with Britain, but maintained their intercourse occasionally with Spain, the languages of these people abound in terms connected with shipping. Cæsar mentions an engagement he had with the combined fleets of the Veneti and Britons, in which the ships are stated to have been built of oaken planks, so firmly constructed that the beaks of the Roman ships could scarce make an impression on them.[1] The usual kind of vessels, however, which were used by the Britons and Irish, were the Cwrwgyl, or Currach, formed of ossier twigs covered with hide; and small boats of this kind, in shape like a walnut-shell, are still used on the rivers of Wales and Ireland. Pliny tells us, that Timæus, a very ancient historian, affirmed that the Britons used to sail to an island at the distance of six days' sail, in boats made of wattles, and covered with skins. Solinus states, that in his time the communication between Britain and Ireland was kept up on both sides by means of these vessels and from Lucan we learn not only that Cæsar took advantage of them, but that they were equally used on the Nile and the Po, as by the Britons.

Besides the Cwrwgyl the Britons had some kind of boat in the very early periods of their history, which they termed Cwch, which seems to have been formed out of a single tree like the Indian canoes.[2]

The land view exhibits the British mode of tilling the ground for the purposes of husbandry, which we are told was with the arad yr arsang, i.e. overtreading plough, and the mattock. This mode was practised by the Egyptians, and is exhibited on the walls of a sepulchre at Eleithias;[3] the man therefore with the mattock has been taken from the same. The figure with the wooden plough, on which he treads to bear it down to the earth by his weight, is taken from an illumination in the British Museum,[4] apparently about the age of the seventh century, and what is extremely remarkable, the cattle which draw the plough are the Uchen banawg, literally hunched oxen, as they are here represented, which do not occur in any later illumination. The overtreading plough was in general use till the middle of the fifth century, when Illtud or Iltutus, according to the Triads, introduced an improved one. Some time, however, must have elapsed before the improvement would be universally adopted, and as Mr. Turner has shewn, the Britons became subjected to the Saxons on their conquest of the country, and subsequently performed all the menial offices, we may fairly venture to assert that this illumination represents a Briton, a British plough, and British buffaloes.

[30]

C.H.S. del.

Aquatinted by R. Havell.

British Fishing, and Husbandry.

[1]Cæsar de Bell. Gall. l. iii. c. 13.

[2]Several of these have been discovered; for an account of which, see King's Munimenta Antiqua, vol. I. p. 29.

[3]See Hamilton's Egyptiaca, pl. xxiii.

[4]A Psalter in Latin version of St. Jerome, Harl. No. 603.

COSTUME OF THE DRUIDICAL ORDER.

The Gentile systems of morality, corrupt and deformed as they became in the later periods of their history, still retained in their more early state something of too pure a nature to be referred to those impious adherents of Nimrod, the Titans. They still cherished some correct ideas of the Deity, derived from the revered patriarch Noah, for the conceptions of the heathen world were darkened by degrees. Abhorring the impiety of the great rebel, and recollecting the punishment of his associates, each society, as it repaired towards its allotted habitation, chose the wisest among them, and those whose characters were unimpeached, to be the instructors of the people, and the depositories of primitive wisdom. Such was the origin of Druidism, and of all the heathen hierarchies.

The original and primitive inhabitants of Britain, at some remote period revised and reformed their national institutes. Their priest or instructor had hitherto been simply named Cwydd or Gydd but it was considered to have become necessary to divide this office between the national or superior priest, and another whose influence should be more limited. From henceforth the former became Der-wydd (Druid), or *superior instructor*, and Go-wydd or O-vydd (Ovate), *subordinate instructor*; and both went by the general name of Beirdd (Bards), or *teachers of wisdom*. As the system matured and augmented, the Bardic order consisted of three classes, the Druids, Beirdd Braint or privileged Bards, and Ovates. The Derwyddon or Druids became peculiarly the ministers of religion, whence the heathenish superstition of the Celtic tribes has been denominated Druidism. To be a Druid it was requisite to have been a Bardd Braint, for this gave him the privilege of presidency. The dress of the Druid was white, the emblem of holiness, and peculiarly of truth, as being the colour of light or the sun,[1] the deity of his peculiar worship.

The figures in this plate are taken from a bas-relief found at Autun, and engraved by Montfaucon in his Antiq. Expliq. They represent two Druids; the one crowned with a garland of oak leaves bearing in his hand a sceptre, denoting his superior rank and office of Arch-Druid.[2] The other is a Druid exhibiting the Cornan or Crescent, termed by the Irish Cead-Rai-Re, or the first quarter of the moon,[3] which in that state was a symbol of the sacred ship, or Ark of Noah, and an ensign of the same import as the Cwrwg Cwydrin, or boat of glass, which Taliesin speaks of as "exhibited in the hand of the stranger," and procuring his admission to the nocturnal celebration. The Druid also holds it to signify that the sixth day of the moon, and consequently the time of the festival, had arrived. Beneath are a Cead-Rai-Re of gold dug up in Ireland, taken from the Collectanea de Rebus Hibernicis, and the golden hook for tearing down the Misseltoe from the oak.

---

[1]Ibid. Taliesin calls it "the proud white garment which separated the elders from the youth." Several French authors assert, that the white garments of the Druids had a purple border.

[2]Cæsar says, "over all these Druids there is one president who enjoys supreme authority among them:" again, "upon his death if any of the survivors excels the rest in dignity, he succeeds; but if several have equal pretensions, the president is chosen by the votes of the Druids." Bell. Gall. lib. vi. c. 13.

[3]Pliny expressly says the Druids paid particular attention to the sixth day of the moon's age.

C.H.S. del.ⁿ   Aquatinted by R. Havell.

Costume of the  *Druidical Order.*

C.H.S. delt.

Aquatinted by R.Havell.

Costume of the Druidical Order.

A BRITISH BARD AND OVATE

Sitting on a rock and attending to the observation of an Ovate who points to the Tau-formed oak, a British Bard is here represented. The Bardd-Braint possessed the principal power of the Bardic order, exclusive of the religious functions; and after presiding at three Gorseddau or conventions, he was denominated Bardd Gorseddawg, and then became fully qualified to exercise all his rights. He could proclaim and hold a Gorsedd, admit disciples and Ovyddion; was capable of being employed in embassies; in the office of herald; and to instruct youth in the science of music, in the laws and the principles of morality. Graduates of this class were denominated Trwyddedawg Braint; and the distinguishing dress of the whole class was the uni-coloured robe of sky-blue, being emblematic of peace, as well as of truth from having no variety of colours.[1] The Telyn (so called from its resemblance to the ribs as they appear on one side of a carcase) or harp, represented in this plate, is taken from an ancient one given in Ledwich's Antiquities of Ireland. Diodorus Siculus says, the Bards of Britain chaunted their poems to the sound of instruments. The original British harps were strung with hair, and consisted probably of the same number of strings as the ribs of the human body, viz. twelve; and such harps were used at first by scholars so late as the tenth century.

The Ovydd was the third order, being an honarary degree, to which the candidate could be immediately admitted without being obliged to pass through the regular discipline required for the others. The requisite qualifications were in general, an acquaintance with valuable discoveries in science, the use of language, letters, astronomy (whence they were called Scronyddion, the Saronides of Diodorus), medicine, and the like. A knowledge of, and genius for poetry, as in the Bardic order, was sometimes looked for, but dispensed with in consideration of other eminent qualifications. The dress of the Ovydd was green, the symbol of learning, as being the colour of the clothing of nature. The robe of the figure in the plate has attached to it the cucullus or hood, the Rheno of the Roman writers, and his staff has a golden top.

[1] Owen's Elegies of Llywarch Hên. Thus Cynddelw, in his ode on the death of Cadwallon, calls them "Wearers of long blue robes."

C.H.S. del.ᵈ

Aquatinted by R.Havell.

A British Bard  *and an Ovate.*

BARDIC SCHOLARS.

The figures in this plate are an Awenydd or Bardic disciple, and a candidate for that initiatory order. The former having been admitted wears a variegated dress of the Bardic colours, blue, green, and white; while the candidate retains his original habit. To be admitted as a scholar, it was necessary that the candidate be of a noble family, and of unimpeached morals. He was seldom initiated into any thing considerable till his understanding, affections, morals, and principles in general, had undergone severe trials. During his probationary state of discipline he was to learn such verses and adages as contained the maxims of the institution, and to compose others himself on any relative subject, doctrinal or moral. The youths here represented are taken from specimens of Gaulish sculptures given by Montfaucon. In the right hand of the disciple is a cup, which it is conjectured contained some of the sacred juice, the *Gwîn a bragawd*, "wine and bragget," or perhaps only the mead drank at great festivals; and in his left a bird, the symbol of an aspirant, for such Taliesin mystically says he was, when speaking of his initiation. Mr. Davies, however, conceives that that bird was the Dryw, a name implying both a wren and a Druid: and if such be correct, the bird here represented cannot be this symbol, for it is a nearer resemblance to a dove. The dove was the bird of good omen, as the raven was that of bad, among the nations of antiquity, the former having returned to Noah with the olive sprig of peace, when the latter wholly deserted him. The other youth has under one arm a pig, and in the hand of the other a box, perhaps to contain its food. The pig was also a symbol of Druidism. The Druids are frequently termed Swine, the Lunar-arkite goddess is as often alluded to under the character of a mystical sow; and the bard Merddin commences his address to a disciple with the words *Oian porchellan*, "listen, little pig." The garment of this lad has been coloured red on the authority of the following lines:

> "Roma magis fuscis vestibus, Gallia *rugis*,
> Et placet hic *pueris* militibusque color."

He wears two garments, one above the other, and it is remarkable that one sleeve is considerably wider than the other.

In the back ground are some British cabbins, the form of which is taken from those of the natives of New Caledonia given by Labillardiere in Pl. 38 of his voyage, as they seem to come nearest to the account left us of the Gaulish houses by Strabo. 'They build their houses of wood in the form of a circle, with lofty tapering roofs,' which, Diodorus says, were of straw; and Cæsar informs us that the British houses resembled those of Gaul.

Bardic  *Scholars.*

IRISH OLLAMH AND HERALDIC BARD.

In Ireland very opposite sentiments seem to have been entertained with regard to the colours of dress to what were held in Britain. Instead of expressing simplicity by an unicolured robe, the Druidic order in Ireland manifests their rank and power by the number of colours of which their habit was composed. By a sumptuary law called Ilbreachta, and referred to Tighernmas, that is, to very near the time of the first arrival of the Milesian colony, the peasantry and soldiers were to have their garments of one colour only, the officers two, the commanders of clans three, Beatachs or Bruighnibs four, the nobles five, the Ollamhs or dignified philosophers six, and the royal family seven. The dress therefore of the Irish Bards in general was composed of a plaided Cota, or one of linen dyed a saffron colour, as represented in the plate before us, and ornamented with needle-work according to the rank of the wearer. This was open before, came down to mid-thigh, and fastened with a girdle round the waist; having sleeves reaching to the wrists. Over this was the cochal, a kind of long cloak reaching as low as the ankles, and fringed at the borders like shagged hair, having affixed to it a hood curiously ornamented with needle-work. The colours were wrought in stripes on the mantle, and consisted of white, blue, green, and red, to which the Ollamhs added purple, thus making six, with the yellow of their tunic. In common they wore on their heads the Barrad or conical cap, but on festivals the Tiaras; they also wore trowsers. This plate not only represents one so clad, but also a Filidhe or herald-bard, similar to the Arvydd-vardd of the Britons. These were arrayed in white flowing robes, the emblem of peace, in allusion to their functions as ambassadors and interposers betwixt hostile tribes, and they usually carried with them their harps.

In the back is a view of that curious Arkite memorial, the ship temple in the county of Mayo. This is situated on a conical hill. Its walls, though without cement, are two feet thick, while its elevation to the roofing is seven. The length of the room it forms within is twenty-five feet; but its breadth is unequal, the groundplan making a curvilinear triangle. The door is placed on one side, in allusion to that in the Ark, a circumstance noticed by almost all heathen nations. This is constructed of three large stones, two converging uprights with an impost. The roof is composed of large flag stones with a grassy covering.

C.H.S. del.t

Aquatinted by R. Havell.

Irish Ollamh, and  *an Heraldic Bard.*

Published June 1,1815, by R. Havell, 3, Chapel Street, London.

A JUDICIAL DRUID.

This plate represents an Arch-Druid in his judicial habit. He is clothed in a stole of virgin white, over a closer robe of the same, that is fastened by a girdle on which appears the crystal of augury, encased in gold. Round his neck is the Jodhain Morain, or breast-plate of judgment, said in the Irish fables to possess the power of squeezing the neck on the utterance of a false judgment, below which appears suspended the Glain neidr or serpent's jewel, and on his head the tiara, also of gold. On one finger of the right hand is a ring, and on another the Iogh-Draoch, chain-ring of divination, while the hand rests on the *Peithynin* or Elucidator, which consisted of several staves or coelbrenau, i.e. omen-sticks, on which the judicial or other maxims were cut, and which being put into a frame were turned at pleasure, so that each stave represented a triplet, when formed of three sides, or a stanza when squared. This stands on a stone altar, before which, coming from his box of straw, appears the holy snake, about to partake of the sacred beverage offered him. This has been introduced in conformity to the description of Taliesin, who represents the Arch-Druid in the sanctuary "whilst the dragon moves round over the places which contain the drink-offering;" and that such was the practise of the ancients, many antiques preserved by Montfaucon evince. On the altar lies one of those curious double pateras of gold, of which so many have been dug up in Ireland; and which Aneurin describes as one of the curved horns that used to be carried on all sides of the shrine of the Helio-arkite God, and which he again tells us were for the drink-offerings. Another vessel of libation found in Ireland is also standing on this stone, and near it a branch of the sacred misseltoe.

In this plate, therefore, it has been attempted to represent the Arch-Druid in his judicial character, about to exhibit, according to Strabo, "his profound knowledge in the laws of his country, for which reason all disputes were referred to his arbitration, whether private and domestic, or public and civil; and from whose decree there was no appeal;" and the whole scene is in the *abditis saltibus*, inaccessible forests, of Mela.

Beneath is a representation of the Iodhan Morain, found twelve feet below the surface of a turbary in the county of Limerick, made of thin plated gold, and neatly chased.

C.H.S. delt.   Aquatinted by R.Havell.

An Arch Druid in  *His Judicial Habit.*

Published June 1, 1815, by R.Havell, 3 Chapel Street, London.

GRAND CONVENTIONAL FESTIVAL OF
THE BRITONS.

The superstition of the Druids corresponded with that of the world in general, not only in its theology, but also in the ceremonies by which the deities were worshipped. The penetrating and accurate Cæsar, marking this similarity, does not hesitate to affirm that they adored Mercury, Apollo, Mars, Jupiter, and Minerva, adding: de his eandem fere, quam reliquæ gentes, habent opinionem, "their opinion respecting these nearly coincides with that of other nations"[1] Dionysius informs us, that the rites of Bacchus were duly celebrated in the British Islands,[2] and Strabo cites the authority of Artemidorus, that "in an island close to Britain, Ceres and Proserpine are venerated with rites similar to the orgies of Samothrace."[3] As it is then an historical fact that the mythology and rites of the Druids were the same in substance with those of the Greeks and Romans, as well as of other nations which came under their observation, we shall have pretty good authorities for the representation of them, if with the ancient Bardic poems in our hands we attentively scrutinize the mythological sculptures of the Egyptians to assist in the composition.[4]

This plate therefore represents Stonehenge, the Gwaith Emreis, ambrosial work, of the ancient Britons, in its original splendour, and decked out for the celebration of the Helio-arkite ceremonies. Stone circles in Ireland are called Caer Sidi;[5] the British Bards apply the same appellation. But this is also the name of the zodiac, and as these temples were constructed on astronomical principles, they either represented that celestial zone, solar cycles of sixty, and thirty stones, or the lunar one of nineteen. But these temples had reference to the terrestrial as well as celestial objects of adoration, and therefore typified the ark, which Taliesin particularly terms Caer Sidi, "the enclosure of the just man."[6] As that sacred vessel contained all the animated world, so this, its representative, was, in reference to it, called "the mundane circle of stones."[7]

This Mawr Côr Cyvoeth, "great sanctuary of dominion,"[8] is represented as it probably appeared "on the morn after May-eve, when the song of the Cuckoo convened the appointed dance over the green,"[9] when "it was rendered complete by the rehearsal" of ancient lore, the chaunting of "hymns" in honour of the British divinities, and the interpretation of their will by the birds of the mountain."[10] At this time the huge stones of the oval adytum, which represented the mundane egg, "were covered with veils," on which were delineated the history of "the dragon king". On the principal trilithon of these appeared "the gliding king with expanding wings, before whom the fair one retreats,"[11] or Jupiter in the form of a dragon about to violate Proserpine, and become the father of Bacchus. On another the serpent entwining two phalli, representing the sun entering the sign Gemini. On a third again the serpent between the sun and moon, shewing that both are affected by eclipses.[12] Similar devices were exhibited on others. Thus was pourtrayed "Hu the distributer, as presiding in the mundane circle of stones, the glaring Hu, the sovereign of Heaven, the gliding king, the dragon, the victorious Beli, Lord of the honey island of Britain;[13] and

C.H.S. del.

Aquatinted by R. Havell.

Grand Conventional Festival of the Britons.

now we see "rapidly moving in the course of the sky, in circles, in uneven numbers, Druids, and Bards unite in celebrating their (dragon) leader."[14]

Taliesin[15] describes the preparation for the solemn periodical rite performed on this day, viz. the removing of the shrine out of the cell in the Arkite island, which seems to have been surrounded only at high water. In his account we may remark a ritual observation of the time of flood, alluding to the deluge; a fanatical rite of piercing the thigh so as to draw blood; and a ceremonial adorning of the sacred rock, which was at that time to display the countenance of the Arkite god. Again, that this was done at the dawn, that the Helio-arkite god might be coming forth from the cell at the precise hour of the sun's rising. That this rock was the chief place of tranquillity, for here the divinity was supposed to reside, excepting at the time of the solemn procession; and lastly, that this patriarchal god, the supreme proprietor, was he who received his family exiled from the world into his ark or sanctuary. Aneurin thus details the different days' ceremonies; "In the festival on the eve of May they celebrate the praise of the holy ones (the helio, and lunar-arkite deities) in the presence of the purifying fire, which was made to ascend on high. On Tuesday they wear their dark garments (in allusion to the darkness of the ark, during the patriarch's confinement). On the Wednesday they purified their fair attire, (typifying Noah's restoration to light). On the Thursday they truly performed their due rites. On the Friday the victims were conducted round the circle. On the Saturday their united exertions were displayed without the circular dome. On the Sunday the men with red blades were conducted round the circle, and on the Monday the banquet was served."[16] In the festival of May-eve, however, the more immediate rites of the Lunar-arkite goddess took place, as those of the solar divinity did in the morning. Thus Taliesin, speaking of the cows which drew her chest, exclaims, "Eminent is the virtue of the free course when the dance is performed. Loud is the horn of the lustrator, when the kine move in the evening."[17] But from the Egyptian sculptures we are led to suppose that her shrine also accompanied that of the Helio-arkite god on the following morning. On this glorious morn the Druids welcomed the rising sun, the Rhwyv Trydar or "leader of the din," with frantic shouts of joy, accompanied with a vocal hymn and instrumental music, and during this "the priests" within the adytum "moved sideways round the sanctuary, whilst the sanctuary was earnestly invoking the gliding king."[18] Just behind the altar appears the presiding Druid, "with the circle of ruddy gems on his golden shield,"[19] the image of the Caer Sidi. This he occasionally struck with the thyrsus or "bush-topped spear,"[20] to have probably the same effect as the horrid din with which the heathens pretended to save the moon at the hour of her eclipse. He presides in the bloody area of the altar, about, in his character of Ysadawr or sacrificer, to slay the victim.[21] Behind are his attendants "overshading the Bardic mysteries with the banners of the Bards."[22] Near at hand is "the spotted cow," in whose collar are entwined "the stalks of the plants about to be drenched with gore, which procured blessings. On a serene day she bellowed (as a warning presage of the deluge), and afterwards she was boiled" or sacrificed.[23] To the left appears "a Bard seated on a grey steed, as governor of the festival."[24] A thick-maned steed is under the thigh of the fair youth, his shield light and broad hangs upon the slender courser. His blue and unspotted weapon (hasta pura) was the assuager of tumult,"[25] being the emblem of peace. "This spear of quartered ash he sometimes extended from his hand over the stone cell of the sacred fire,"[26] as he rode about the temple. Conspicuous in the centre stands the "bull or brindled ox with the thick head-band, having seven score knobs on his collar."[27] This animal was the symbol of the patriarch in his character of husbandman. It was attended by three priests termed Garan hîr, lofty cranes, from their attendance also on the water mysteries. Hence this deity was called Tarw Trigaranau, "Tarvos Trigaranos," and sculptured with three cranes on his back.[28] This animal in the Triads is termed "the yellow ox of the spring," in commemoration of the sign Taurus, into which the sun entered at the season when the Druids celebrated the great arkite mysteries; the brown ox which stopped the channel, from the promise which Noah obtained that no future deluge should occur; and the brindled ox with the thick head-band. Such is the "animal which the-silver headed ones" or hoary Druids "protect."[29] In front of this is another symbol of the divinity, "the eagle raised aloft in the sky in the path of Granwyn" or Apollo (the ecliptic) "before the pervading sovereign" or rising sun.[30]

Such appears the temple within; but Taliesin asks, "Who approaches the Caer with white dogs, (Druids,) and large horns?[31] We must therefore examine the grand procession.

First of this band appears the divining Bard with his hudwydd or magic wand, followed by the Bards striking their tuneful harps[32] whose number was sometimes "seven score."[33] Next follows the shrine of Ceridwen, or "curvatures of Kyd (the ark) which passed the grievous waters, stored with corn, and is borne aloft by serpents" or attendant priests. On the preceding eve this shrine had been drawn by cows and attended by torch-bearers, whence Ceres was represented as having wandered over the earth with lighted torches. Now it is attended only by three priests, the Hierophant, who represented "the great creator;" – "one bearing a torch," who personated the sun, and the herald, who as the especial minister of the goddess was regarded as a symbol of the moon.[34] Next comes "the house" or shrine of the Helio-arkite god, "recovered from the swamp," which is preceded by "the assembled train, dancing after their manner, and singing in cadence, some with garlands" of ivy "on their brows,"[35] others with cornute caps. "These are the oxen of Hu the mighty, with part of his chain," the symbol of his confinement, and his five attendants, which we now behold with golden harness of active flame."[36] These have drawn the Avanc or huge monster from the lake, during which the attendants sing a piece of music still known to a few persons in Wales, called "Cainc yr Ychain banawg," which was an imitation of the lowing of the oxen, and the rattling of chains.[37] The hunched oxen which the Druids employed in this rite were probably of the finest breed which the country afforded, but distinguished either by the size of their horns, or some peculiar mark, and set apart for sacred use. They are now drawing the Avanc to where Taliesin intimates the diluvian patriarch found rest, viz. the spot on which the spotted cow was sacrificed. Originally three oxen drew the Avanc, and probably represented the sons of the patriarch; but as Ham incurred the displeasure of his father, so one is said to have been unequal to the task, and consequently left behind. But "the two oxen of distinguished honour put their necks under the car of the lofty one. Majestic were they, with equal pace they moved to the festival."[38] Thus we see the Avanc was the car or shrine of the Diluvian god which was drawn from the lake or representative deluge to his temples and sanctuaries upon firm ground, by which he was invested with the empire of the recovered eath. These yoked oxen also refer to the deity himself; for Taliesin, speaking in his name, says, "I was subjected to the yoke for my affliction, but commensurate was my confidence, the world had no existence were it not for my progeny."[39] "This house, recovered from the swamp, is surrounded with crooked horns," some of the dancers before carrying the double pateras, and those who follow sounding "loud the horns of the lustrator." It is also followed by others bearing "crooked swords in honour of the mighty king of the plains," and the whole is closed by the "circular revolutions performed by the attendants and white bands in graceful extravagance," and those "with curved swords and clattering shields."[40]

On the rampart surrounding the temple are assembled the representatives of the people, the heads of tribes and families, with their standard bearers,[41] while the people themselves, who, Cæsar says, "nullo adhibetur concilio," were never admitted into the assemblies, are viewing the procession in groups on the plains.

Beneath is the ground-plan of the serpentine temple at Abury.

[1]The Helio-arkite god of the Britons was a Pantheos; as Gwyddon Ganhebon, the inventor of the arts and sciences, and as Hu, the conductor of the primitive race, he was Mercury and Hercules; as Beli or the solar divinity, he was Apollo; as Cadwaladyr, the supreme disposer of battle, he was Mars; as Ior, the sovereign of heaven, he was Jupiter; as the giver of wine and generous liquor, and as president of festive carousals, he was Bacchus; as Nevydd Nav Neivion, the celestial lord of the waters, he was Neptune; as Saidi or Sadwrn, he was Saturn; as Morion, with the two faces, he was Janus, &c. In the same manner the Lunar-arkite goddess, as Ogyrven amhad, goddess of seeds, was Ceres, she was Diana, Proserpine, Venus, Andraste, &c.

[2]Perieg. vol. 565, &c.

[3]Lib. iv.

[4]See particularly Hamilton's Egyptiaca, pl. xxiv.

[5]O'Connor's Dissertation on the Hist. of Ireland.

[6]Poem on the Spoils of the Deep.

[7]Taliesin's peom on Uthur Pendragon. Aneurin and Merddin also speak of the stones which composed the circular temples.

[8]Poem of Cuhelyn, Gwaith Emreis likewise implies "the structure of the revolution," and the letters which form this name when valued as Celtic or Greek numerals, mark the day (viz. 366,) on which that revolution is completed by the sun.

[9]Taliesin on the praise of Lludd the Great.

[10]Taliesin's Mic Dinbych, or view of the Bardic sanctuary.

[11]Taliesin's elegy on Uthyr Pendragon, i.e. wonderful supreme dragon, or leader.

[12]Dramatic representations of a similar hieroglyphic nature seem to have been common in India: thus the Rev. Mr. Maurice asks, "What are the eternal contest of the Soors and Assoors, or bright and sable genii,

represented in the festival dramas of India, especially at the great equinoctial feast of Durga, but emblematical representations of the imagined contests of the summer and winter signs, for the dominion of the varied year, and the different aspects of the planets?" What is meant by the great celestial dragon, that on every eclipse seizes with its teeth the affrighted sun and moon, but the ascending and descending nodes? What is the serpent with a thousand heads on which Vishnu sleeps at the solstitial period, but the hydra of the skies, that vast constellation, the numerous stars enclosed in which are poetically called its flaming heads, vomiting fire, and on which the Greeks founded the story of the Lernæan hydra, slain by Hercules (that is, the constellation Hercules), the foot of which latter asterism, on the celestial sphere, is placed near the head of the former. These dramatic exhibitions at the various festivals of India, nearly all founded upon astronomical observations, &c. I can consider in no other light than as relics of the sacred mysteries, anciently exhibited in the holy grove, and gloomy cavern."

[13]Elegy on Uthyr Pendragon.

[14]Cynddelw's Ode to Owain Cyveilianwg.

[15]In his Ox-pen of the Bards.

[16]Gododin, xxiv.

[17]Cadair teyrn On.

[18]Elegy on Uthyr Pendragon.

[19]Taliesin's Cad goddeu or battle of the trees.

[20]Poem of Llywarch ab Llywelyn.

[21]Poem in MS. supposed to be the composition of Aneurin, in Davies's Myth. p. 576.

[22]Cad goddeu.

[23]The praise of Lludd mawr.

[24]Gododin, xxvii.

[25]God. i.

[26]God. xii.

[27]Taliesin's Spoils of the Deep. Some conical knobs of wood covered with a thin plate of gold have been discovered in barrows on Stonehenge with other Druidical insignia (see Arch. vol. xv.), and also in Ireland (Arch. vol. III. pl. xix.), and if these were the same the graves containing them must have belonged to the attendant ministers. They appear however very large, to have amounted to 140, and it is difficult to reconcile this if we even suppose four rows on the collar. This was the number of stones which completed the temple on Salisbury Plain, and Mr. Davies conjectures, they were mystically described as his collar.

[28]See Montfaucon. This bull with his three attendant ministers is observable in the sculpures at Eleithias. See Hamilton's Ægyp. pl. xxiv.

[29]Taliesin's Spoils of the Deep. Merddin also speaks of this sacred ox.

[30]Mic Dinbich.

[31]Dialogue between Ugnach and Taliesin.

[32]Thus Taliesin in his Uthyr Pendragon, says "I am a Bard, I am a master of the harp, the pipe, and the crwth."

[33]Ibid.

[34]Dialogue between Arthur and Cai in the the Welsh Archaiology.

[35]MS. poem following Aneurin's Gododins.

[36]Poem of Llewelyn Moel.

[37]See Owen's Welsh Dict. in voce Banawg.

[38]Gwynvardd Brecheinawg.

[39]Elegy on Uthyr Pendragon.

[40]MS. poem following the Gododins.

[41]The following names of persons are derived from their office of ensign-bearers, Cynllo, calf's-head; Cyntwrch, hog's head; Cynvarch, horse's head; Cynwalsh, hawk's head, &c. Lewis Morris's letters in Camb. Reg.

BOADICEA, QUEEN OF THE ICENI.

We are now arrived at the period coeval with the residence of the Romans in Britain, and in contemplating the dress of this time the first specimen that occurs is that of the Queen of the Iceni.

Of Boadicea or Aregwedd *Voeddug*, i.e. the victorious, as she was styled by her countrymen, of which epithet the Romans latinized a name for her, ancient authors have been studious to preserve a particular description. Comparing therefore the accounts of Strabo with those of Dion Cassius, and by carefully examining the dresses of the Celtic females on the columns of Trajan and Antonine, the basso-relievos found in this country, and the coins of Carausius, there is little difficulty in delineating the costume of this princess. Accordingly this plate represents her as a full-grown handsome woman, but of a stern countenance, with long yellow[1] hair flowing over her shoulders. She wears the Pais much longer than what was worn by the men, hence that word is now confined to designate the petticoat. It is woven chequerwise of many colours, which, according to Strabo and Pliny, were purple, light and dark red, violet and blue. Over this is the shorter garment, open on the bosom, and with short sleeves exposing the arms,[2] termed Gwn, the Gaunacum of Varro, which reached as far as the knee, also of interwoven colours. On her shoulders was thrown her cloak, fastened by a fibula, and from her neck depended a golden torque. Bracelets ornamented her arms and wrists, and rings her fingers. This was her usual habit, says Dion. At the back are seen the Britons busily employed in their warlike preparations, and the Petoritum of the queen containing her daughters, one of whom is in sight.[3]

Beneath is represented a very curious ancient British female relic, being no less than a pair of bronze breast plates, discovered on ploughing a field near the top of Polden Hill, Somersetshire. The diameter of each is 10¾ inches, and the weight 4¼ ounces.

---

[1]Whether this was flaxen hair, or discoloured by the chalky lixivium, is not mentioned.

[2]Tacitus de Mor. Germ. c. 17. Though this was said of the German women, it is equally applicable to those of Britain.

[3]Of the two warriors behind the car, one has a crested, and the other a horned helmet. The former is taken from a head on a coin with the legend COM, attributed to Comius king of the Atrebatæ, engraved by Bejer, and the other from one in Montfaucon's Antiq. Expliq.

Boadicea, Queen *of the Iceni.*

A ROMANIZED BRITON AND A FERYLLT.

The figures in this plate are taken, one from a sculpture, and the other from a British coin. Antiquaries are all agreed that the bas-relief represents a Romanized Briton in his cloak and Sagum, and we have therefore made the former a plaid, while the latter has the usual red colour of that Gaulish habit. This interesting stone was found at Ludgate, in London, A.D. 1669, and is preserved at Oxford amongst the Arundelian marbles. It proves that in a few years after the erection of the British towns, and in the progress of refinement, the ancient habit began to be disesteemed by the British chiefs, and regarded as the badge of ancient barbarism. Thus Tacitus observed, "the sons of the British chieftains began to affect our dress;" and forcibly painted how strongly the adoption of the less manly habits, as well as effeminate manners tended to rivet their chains. The Briton here represented has a Cleddyv deuddwrn, or two-handed sword.

The Feryllt is taken from the third of the plates of British coins in Gough's edition of Camden's Britannia. He has wrapped round him his garment of the Ovate's colour; and between his legs an anvil in which one impression of the die is cut while the other had been engraved in his hammer: "having therefore caused his furnace to boil without water, and prepared the solid metal to endure for the age of ages," he holds it in the pincers over the die in the anvil, and strikes it at the same time with the hammer.

At the feet of the Feryllt are seen a variety of implements of his manufacture, such as a bit, several sorts of axe-heads, a mould for casting chip-axes, and a scythe for the axles of the war chariots.

Below is the coin from which this subject has been taken, and also one from Speed, representing a mounted British slinger.

C.H.S. del.   Aquatinted by R. Havell.

A Romanised Briton, and a *Feryllt.*

ROMAN-BRITISH FEMALES.

If the men followed so readily the Roman fashions, we have no reason to think from modern experience that the ladies would not be as anxious to adopt whatever was new in the article of dress; and yet the specimens here given are so nearly allied to those of the Britons of the present day, that we are surprised at the resemblance. The left-hand figure, with her head wrapped somewhat in the Irish mode, is taken from the reverse of a coin of Carausius, the other from a basso-relievo found in Somersetshire.[1] They are both habited in the Gwn and Pais, just like the Welsh peasantry of the present time, except that the former, instead of opening before and wrapping over, appear of the shirt-like form, and consequently copies of the Roman tunic.

Beneath is a Roman medal, struck on the conquest of Britain by the Emperor M. Aurelius Antoninus Pius, which represents a trophy composed of British spoils, and gives us the male and female attire of the Britons at that period.[2]

[1]See Horsley's Brit. Rom. Somersetshire, No. iv. Amabinogi informs us that the British Olwen or Venus was said to be arrayed in a vesture of flance-coloured silk. The coin of Carausius from which the first female is taken, is in the plate of Roman coins, in Gough's Camden, vol. I. page cxviii. No. 19.

[2]See Gough's Camden, vol. I. plate of Roman coins, No. 14. All the Brito-Roman coins and basso-relievos agree in exhibiting the tunic as worn over the pais, with sleeves, as at the present day in Wales, descending only down to the elbows.

C.H.S. del.t

Aquatinted by R.Havell.

Roman British *Females.*

Published June 1.1815, by R.Havell, 3, Chapel Street, London.

ROMAN-BRITISH PRIESTESSES.

These figures represent two Roman-British priestesses, one in her ancient, and one in the assumed Roman dress. The isles and islands of the British Seas which were deemed sacred, and in which the mysteries of Ceridwen were performed, are frequently termed by the bards Caer Sëon, sacred enclosures of the Sëon or British priestesses. Mela had heard of one of these, and thus speaks of it: "Sena situated in the British sea, over against the land of the Osismii, is famous for the oracle of a Gaulish deity, whose priestesses, devoted to perpetual virginity, are said to be nine in number. They are called Galli-cenæ, supposed to be of great genius and rare endowments; capable of raising storms by their incantations, of transforming themselves into what animals they please, of curing ailments reckoned by others beyond the reach of medicine; quick at discerning and able to foretel what is to come; but easy of address only to sailors, and to those who come into this island on purpose to consult them."

The female deity, and consequently her priestesses, had also the name of Bronwen or "white-breast," a title that induces the supposition that they did not study to conceal so fascinating a part of their persons, and it is therefore probable that the left-hand figure gives the exact appearance which these Tylwyth têg, or fair society, as they were also called, exhibited. It is taken from some sculptures found in Northumberland,[1] the head-dresses of which being defaced, this is represented from a coin. The other female, except her hair, which is dressed in the true British style,[2] has more the Roman appearance, and therefore affords a specimen of a Roman-British Priestess in the latter time of the residence of the Romans in Britain. It is taken from a bas-relief found at Elenborough in Cumberland, which Dr. Horsley conjectures represented the goddess Setlocenia. The singularity in the habit of this female is the zig-zag or Vandyke borders, affected probably because equilateral triangles typified the elements, and as such were deemed fit ornaments for Druidical tiaras, crescents, pateræ, and other implements.

The back-ground represents the temples of Minerva and Sul-Minerva at Bath, restored from the vignette to Lyson's Roman antiquities of that city. That it was once very magnificent, we learn from Solinus, who describing it says, "in quo spatio fontes calidi opiparo exculti apparatu ad usus mortalium."

Beneath is a British coin, which exhibits the mode in which the ladies of this isle, and more particularly perhaps those attached to the service of religion, adorned their hair.

---

[1]Horsley's Brit. Rom. Northumberland, pl. 19, No. 48, 49, and 50, also Yorkshire. Dr Horsley takes the figures found at Houseteads in Northumberland to be three Sortes. There are several other representations of them all seated, having their legs, bosoms, and arms bare. One among them is represented bound with cords. Qu. Does this exhibit a Së designed for destruction, or in the momment of inspiration? The fact of nine of these females having been discovered at this station, seems to corroborate the idea of their being the Sëon; and the Doctor himself acknowledges that they might have been local deities.

[2]See the heads on the British coins, and Lady Moira's letter in the seventh vol. of the Arch.

C.H.S. del.ᵗ

Aquatinted by R. Havell.

Roman British Priestesses.

Published June 1. 1815, by R. Havell, 3, Chapel Street, London.

IRISH BREHONS.

It had been our hope to have given in this place a specimen of the dress of the ancient Picts, whose warlike incursions occasioned so much annoyance to the Romans. The source from which we should have derived our authority, is a brick discovered at Cambridge, of which the vignette at the bottom of the plate is a representation; but there are too many suspicious circumstances attached for us to deem it sufficiently authentic. Had our grounds been sufficient to rely on, we should have traced the filleadh-beg or petticoat (certainly not of Celtic origin) to that people; but as it is, we must suppose them to have derived it from the Romans.[1]

We are therefore obliged to substitute for our sixteenth plate, specimens of the dress of the Irish Brehons, or Judges, a class on whom, at a later period, was conferred the Druidical privilege of hearing and determining causes, public and private, according to the known laws of the country.

[1]The Picts are first spoken of by the Roman writers, A.D. 297, with the Caledonians. They were, however, of Scandinavian origin, and made their first descent on the Scottish coast about A.D. 50; and became a formidable people in about two centuries afterwards, and assisted occasionally by the Irish, they succeeded in subduing the Maæatae and Caledonians. While some of the Irish by sea infested the Roman province, others uniting with the Picts, forced their way over the Wall, and made themselves known by the name of Scots. Under this title, in 503, they obtained permanent footing in Scotland, and ultimately succeeded in entirely subjugating the Picts to their control.

C.H.S. del.

Aquatinted by R. Havell.

Irish *Brehons.*

COSTUME OF THE PAGAN IRISH.

The subject of this plate is taken from a most curious and valuable fragment of Irish sculpture, a fac-simile of which is given underneath.[1] It is curious as an unique specimen of Irish mythology, and valuable as one of the many corroborations Irish antiquities have afforded to British mystical poems. It represents no less than the initiation into the mysteries of the Helio-arkite religion of these islands, and that very interesting part of them, the completion of the less, and commencement of the greater; while it at the same time affords us authentic examples of the Bardic costumes of Ireland, probably as old as the time of St. Patrick.

In order to explain the subject, we must refer to a very singular piece of British mythology, called Hanes Taliesin, *the History of Taliesin*, or *radiant front*, which details the various ceremonies a candidate for the priesthood underwent; and by a comparison with the mysteries of Ceres, as described by Apulius, and Dion Chrysostom, with other notices of the ancients, we shall at once arrive at its meaning. In order to pass the minor ceremonies, the aspirant was kept for a certain time within a cromlêch, cell, or cave,[2] where he studied the fanatical rites, and imbibed the sacred doctrines of Ceres, or the Lunar-arkite goddess. This inclosure was called the womb of the goddess: and in the Hanes Taliesin, she is symbolized as a greyhound bitch. In a sculpture which, according to De Gebelin, represents the Eleusinian cave, Ceres is attended by a dog, and the aspirant, in the form of a child, is brought into the cave by another dog.[3] Hence Virgil,

"Visæque canes ululare per umbras,"

Plutarch, and others. The British priests, as well as those of Egypt, are often styled dogs; and they and their goddess are, as Plutarch hints, so typified, in allusion to the fidelity, vigilance, and sagacity of that animal. The Hanes Taliesin goes on to state, that after having swallowed the aspirant, "she was pregnant of him nine months, and when delivered of him, she found him so lovely a babe, that she had not resolution to put him to death. She placed him, however, in a coracle, covered with a skin, and, at the instigation of her husband, cast him into the sea on the twenty-ninth of April."[4] The completion of the initiatory rites was deemed by the Gentiles a regeneration, or *new birth*; the representation of the greyhound bitch and babe in this plate, is therefore intended mystically to show that the aspirant had completed his course of discipline in the previous mysteries. He has now to undergo the greater. Plutarch informs us that the second day of the mysteries of Ceres was called 'Αλαδε Μυσται, "Noviciates to the sea," from this being the form in which the herald summoned those who had passed the less to prepare for the greater.[5] In the Hanes Taliesin, the British goddess employs a minister, who is mystically described as a son of a herald: whence it may be implied that he himself held that office,[6] and another is called Morda, i.e. ruler of the sea; or Gwydd-naw, priest of the ship. So in the celebration of the rites of Ceres, we have one priest termed Keryx, or the herald, and another Hydranus, i.e. one whose function was with water. The two figures in this plate therefore represent an heraldic bard, who, pointing to the sum, invokes the noviciate to

C.H.S. del.t

Aquatinted by R. Havell.

Costume of the  *Pagan Irish.*

prepare for the ceremonies in honour of the Helio-arkite divinity, while the priest of the ship, or sea, is about to convey him to the covered coracle, to undergo the mimic representation of the deluge.

As a subject of costume, this plate affords us the dresses of two officiating priests in the habits peculiar to their office. The Hydranus, or minister of the sea, appears in his long stole of virgin white, the uniform and general dress of the Irish Druids previous to the promulgation of the sumptuary law called Ilbreacta, in the time of Tigernmas.[7] The herald is in his Truise, or striped pantaloons, Cotaigh, or tunic of yellow, and variegated Cochal, or hood.[8] This dress, with the addition of a fringed cloak, is represented on the figure of a bard in basso-relievo, that was found in the ruins of New Abbey, near Cilcullen.[9]

In the distance appears a Gowlan, or more properly, a Gollan temple, with the Barr-cheann, or pillar stone, near it. The name still exists in many parts of Ireland, and is noticed in Smith's History of Cork, vol. ii. p. 412.

Beneath is the fragment of a stone, from which the subject of the plate has been taken.

[1]It is taken from a plate in the Collect. de Reb. Hib. vol. vi.

[2]Davies's Mythol. of the Druids. Porphyry de Antro Nymph. and Maurice's Indian Antiq. vol. II.

[3]Monde primitif, tom. IV. p. 336. In the parish of Llanbeudy, Caermarthenshire, there is a cromlêch called Bwrdd Arthur, i.e. the table of Arthur, or the great bear (the mythological diluvian god,) and at the same time Gwâl y Vilast, the couch, or Πϰστος of the greyhound bitch, the genius of the ark. In plate 26 of the second vol. of the Supplement to Montfaucon's Antiquities, are female priestesses, attended by a dog; there are also Victimarii, wearing the bardocucullus, boots, and broaches.

[4]Arch. of Wales, vol. I. p. 17. The Druidicial greater mysteries commenced on May-eve.

[5]Plut. in Vitâ Pho.

[6]Davies's Myth. of the Druids.

[7]Walker's Dress of the Irish, p. 9.

[8]Giraldus Cambrensis speaks of the Cochal or Cucullus in these words: "Caputiis namque modicis assueti sunt et arctis, trans humeros deorsum, cubito tenus protensis variisque colorum generibus panni colorumque consutis."

[9]Walker's Memoirs of the Irish Bards.

HIBERNIAN MALE AND FEMALE COSTUME.

Diodorus the Sicilian gives the following description of the costume of the Celtiberians who inhabited the south-western parts of Spain. "They wear black rough Saga, made of coarse wool, like goat's hair. Some are armed with light Gallic shields, others with circular Cyrtiæ, as big as bucklers, wear greaves about their legs made of rough hair, and brazen helmets upon their heads, adorned with reddish purple crests. They carry two-edged swords exactly tempered with steel, and daggers too, a span long, which they make use of in close fight." Giraldus de Barri, describing the dress of the Irish in the 12th century, informs us "that they were but lightly clad in woollen garments, barbarously shaped, and for the most part black, because the sheep of the country are of that colour." Two-edged swords of brass have been found in Ireland; shields were undoubtedly used by them, probably both oblong and circular; boots of untanned leather, called brogues, they wore for many centuries; and the Irish skian is about a span long. Thus is the description of Celtiberian dress at the same time a strong confirmation that the Irish were of Spanish origin, and a proof of the antiquity of the costume described by Giraldus. This author goes on to state that "the Irish usually wore moderate close caputia, or hooded mantles, covering the shoulders, and reaching down to the elbows, composed of various colours and stripes, for the most part sewed together." This cloak, which in the life of St. Cadoc, written in the 6th century, is termed Coccula, is described as "a sort of garment used by the Irish, on the outside shagged or napped, and woven like braided hair." It differed, however, according to the quality of the wearer, being sometimes of the finest cloth, bordered with fine woollen fringe of scarlet, and other various colours. Many rows of this shag or fringe were sewed on the upper part of the mantle, partly for ornament, and partly to defend the neck from cold, and along the edges ran a narrow fringe of the same texture. Under this cloak, say Giraldus, they have fallins, or jackets, and trowsers forming breeches and hose of one piece. The Irish therefore very nearly resembled the picture Strabo has drawn of the Belgic Gauls.

The indefatigable Speed, by his representations of a wild Irishman, and wild Irishwoman, in the time of King James I., in his topographical account of Ireland, has supplied us with the general idea of the present plate. The male figure is habited in a fallin, and trowsers, his legs and feet covered with the brogues, and his shoulders with a fringed cloak of the platted kind. His temples and beard are shaved, while the hair on the top of the head is collected behind into a single lock, or glib, as it was termed. In his hand he grasps the short lance, in common use in Ireland. The female is altogether copied from Speed; and her costume is evidently of the most antique appearance. She seems to be covered with a large piece of cloth, trimmed with fringe, and perforated in the middle to pass the head through, the opening being likewise adorned with a ruff made of the same kind of fringe. The head is bare, and the feet covered with brogues.

In the distance is seen one of the round towers common in Ireland, which although they are denominated in Irish Cloghad, or belfries, were more probably constructed for watch towers, and also appropriated to religious purposes. This specimen is copied from that at Kildare. It is upwards of 130 feet high, 45 in circumference at the base, and 10 feet in the clear within, and is crowned with a parapet, capable of holding one person only. The sketch beneath represents a golden Aision, or crown, dug up in 1692, in a bog in the county of Tipperary. It weighed five ounces; the border and head were raised in chase-work, and the whole bears a resemblance to the close crown of the eastern empire.

C.H.S. del.t   Aquatinted by R.Havell

Hibernian Male, & *Female Costume.*

PABO POST PRYDAIN.

Pabo, on whom was bestowed the enviable title of "The Pillar of Britain," was the son of Arthwys ab Mor, and the brother of Eliver and Ceidio. He had, as we might have imagined by the epithet recited, distinguished himself greatly in the latter part of the fifth century, in opposing the inroads of the Gwddelian Fichti, or Hibernian Pictish forces, that invaded his territories in the north. But his deeds of valour proving no permanent obstacle to their success, he was compelled to relinquish his Cumbrian lands, and seek refuge in Cambria. Following, however, the fashion of the times, he led a holy life, and became a reputed saint of the British church. His piety led him to bestow his worldly possessions in founding a church in Anglesea, which after him was named Llan-Babo; and here in the time of King Charles II. his tomb, with an inscription, was discovered. A print of it has been preserved by Rowland, in his Mona Antiqua, and from that the representation here given has been made.

He is clad in a long Dalmatic, partly open at the sides, and bordered with fur. Round the neck, and down the front, is a border of lace, richly studded with pearls.

Beneath is a sketch of the tomb-stone itself; a sort of schistus verging into slate, not the produce of Anglesea.

C.H.S. delt.

Aquatinted by R. Havell.

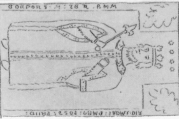

Pabo Post *Prydain.*

SAINT IESTIN AB GERAINT.

This saint, to whom there are two churches dedicated, one in Anglesea, about three miles north-west of Beaumaris, and the other in the south-west part of Caernarvonshire, was the son of that celebrated naval hero, Geraint ab Erbin, a prince of the Devonshire Britons. The saint is habited in a cope, fastened on the breast with a rich fibula: beneath this he has a short mantle or scapular over his tunic. This mode of dress was of the highest antiquity, and remained in vogue for royal personages till the time of Henry V. In his right hand he holds a staff, not unlike the augural staff of the ancients.

In a wood at the back is seen a curiously ornamented cross, now existing by the road side leading to the village of Carew, in Pembrokeshire.

C.H.S. del.^t   Aquatinted by R. Havell.

S^t. Iestin 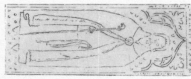 *ab Geraint.*

MILITARY COSTUME OF THE GOTHIC
NATIONS ON THE WESTERN COASTS
OF THE BALTIC.

The Gothic and Sclavonian nations who had intermixed on the western coast of the Baltic, had assimilated their worship, manners, and customs long before they were converted to Christianity. Their roving habits, their piratical disposition, their ideas, prejudices, and institutions, were all similar, and consequently their arms and dresses could differ but little from each other. In the most remote periods there is little doubt that they fought almost entirely destitute of defensive armour; and when they became familiarized with the warlike manners of their more polished neighbours, a high unbending prejudice induced them often to reject every kind of protective arms, as unbecoming the valour of their nature.

The Cymbri, however, while they continued independent, and distinct from these, seem to have worn armour; for they are represented, on their invasion of Gaul, as wearing iron breast-plates, and carrying white shields. They bore as offensive weapons, maces, darts, and swords of unusual forms, and, according to Plutarch, had long swords.[1] Their women, as was the case with their Gaulish and British consanguinei, fought with lances.

At a later period the Saxons and Danes made use of battle-axes, bows, and arrows, and were distinguished by curved short swords, slung by a belt across the right shoulder. This distinctive weapon was the sword known to historians by the name of Saex, or Sais, and was in the form of a scythe.[2] It seems to have been peculiar to the Saxons, and possibly because fighting more constantly on horseback than the Danes, they made this weapon serve both for action, and procuring fodder for their cavalry. The battle-axe was double-edged, or a bipennis, and denominated Byl. Those affixed to long staves were the hallebardes,[3] and were more commonly in the hands of the infantry, who defended their castles, and thence denominated Traband or Trauband, "trusty bands."

In the most ancient chronicles, the Scandinavians are represented as excellent archers; a quality for which the later Saxons do not appear to have been conspicuous. All the northern nations made occasional use of the dart, the sling, the mace armed with points, the hammer, often of flint, the lance, and the dirk or poignard. For defence they bore shields, some of which were of a long oval form, so as to cover a man entirely: these were the *skiold*, the others were in remote periods small, but afterwards considerably larger; they were round, convex, and often furnished with a boss of iron,[4] or other metal. The larger sort were invariably of wood, bark, or leather; the others, and particularly those of the chiefs, were of iron or brass, engraved, painted, or gilt, and sometimes were even covered with a plate of gold. The large shield served also at sea and on shore to carry the wounded or dead, as a shelter against rain, or for an occasional fence. The helmet, though often disregarded, was known to the Scandinavians and Gothic tribes at a very early period; the inferior warriors wearing them of leather,

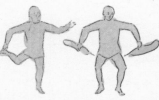

Military Costume   *of the Gothic Nations,*
    on the Western Coasts   *of the Baltic.*

C.H.S. del.^t

Aquatinted by R.Havell.

and the chiefs of iron, or metal gilt. The breast-plate was also not unknown; and in the eighth century, the chiefs appear to have had them of iron, shaped somewhat like those of the Romans. The scaly and ring mail[5] were probably introduced and rendered common by the Sarmatian tribes, who settled near the Baltic after the Vandals had departed. Warriors usually wore torques; and over their armour they sometimes hung surcoats of peltry, or cloth. Their lower limbs were covered with close trowsers; and in their boots or brogues they put dried grass to keep the feet warm, as the peasantry of many countries do at this day. When wearing shoes, this grass was wound round the ankles, until the substitution of cloth gave origin to the fashion of cross gartering.

The warriors here represented are taken from one of the celebrated horns of gold found at Galhuus, in the earldom of Skakkenberg, in Denmark.[6] They exhibit the dress of heroes, gods, or Berserkir. The first, who appears from his superior stature and straight sword to be a Dane, has a small skull-cap on his head, with a nasal or point to protect the face. His armour seems to be of leather, the lower part of which is covered by a sort of surcoat of fur, or some striped material, such as Aneurin, the Welsh bard, observed in the dress of Octa. His shield is small, convex, and adorned with a star of eight points, which ornament is again pictured on his breast. Next to this warrior is another in similar armour, but without surcoat. His breast-plate is evidently of two pieces, which appears to be connected by the buttons on the breast.[7] His shield is still smaller than that of the other, and he holds in the same hand a kind of knife, which is broad and blunt at its end. This may possibly distinguish him as a Sclavonian race. His cap is singularly distinguished by two long feathers; a practice still in vogue with the Tartar warriors.[8]

At the feet of these figures are seen a Saxon sword,[9] and a battle-axe; and in the distance of a Saxon horseman in the same armour, and another dressed in a short tunic, who bears a shield and sword something like a modern table-knife. At the bit of his horse are several large rings.

Below is represented the Saxon pastime of dancing between swords. All these figures are copied from the golden horns; the two last, without alteration, in the attitudes, or drawing.

[1]These were the Degan or Spad, so highly prized, as to be sometimes, on account of their cruciform shape, the symbol of the Deity. They were sharp, and often inscribed with Rhunic characters; and in order to create greater terror, those of the chiefs had proper names. See Mallet's Introd.

[2]The word *Sais*, in the lower Saxon modern dialect, still signifies that implement of husbandry.

[3]Alle-bard, "cleave-all," or Helle-bard, "Flat cleaver."

[4]Many of these have been found in barrows in England. The Anglo-Saxon shields are generally embellished with rows of studs in the form of a star.

[5]See Sarmatians thus accoutred on the Trajan column. Aneurin tells us that Hengist was "clad in scaly mail."

[6]The first was found in 1639, the second in 1734. This last is upwards of 7 lbs. weight, though a part is broken off. They are both of fine gold. The horn of 1639 is represented in the frontispiece to this work. It has numerous figures of warriors, gods, animals, and monsters engraved on it, several of which figures are here

given. From its Rhunic inscription, it is evident that some of the Roman letters had already been admitted into their alphabet, yet none of the Scandinavian antiquaries have been able to read it. This circumstance, however, gives a sort of date to this curious horn; and considering the richness of the material, and the beauty of the workmanship, it is possible that the little republic of Jomsberg was the spot where this and similar costly instruments were manufactured. This conjecture derives additional strength, from the representation of Trigla upon it, the favourite divinity of the Jomsberg Scandinavians.

[7] Several of these double buttons, composed of metal, have been found in Danish barrows, and are in Pontoppidan's collection. Some Anglo-Saxon drawings represent these corselets of three and four pieces, in circles round the body, and painted of various colours, as is also asserted in the 15th Gododin.

[8] The Tartars still use eagles' plumes. The Scottish chief represented in the Ancient Costume of England has evidently a similar ornament in his helmet.

[9] A sword somewhat similar is still preserved in the Tower. Captain Smith once possessed a Moorish sword of the same description. It was not quite so much curved as those represented in the plate, and of a size that might have been concealed in a wide sleeve, as was done by Hengist's followers at the massacre of the Britons. The form of this Moorish weapon may be a relic of the Goths when they were in Africa.

A DROTTE AND A FOLA.

The religious institutions of the Cimbric Scandinavians were originally similar to those of all the other Celtic nations inhabiting the west of Europe, making some allowances for the difference of climate, and consequently of manners, the poverty and still greater state of barbarism to which they were reduced. By the invasion of the first Scythian or Sclavonian conquerors, led by the man who had assumed the sacred name of the Gothic deity, a great mixture of other rites seem to have been introduced, some supposed to have originated in eastern Tartary, others on the confines of Persia. Of both these modes of worship, and their peculiar rites, the wild incoherent poems of the Edda, the mythological productions of the Welsh and Irish bards, and the Scandinavian Saga, have left sufficient traces, and to this day Sweden and Denmark contain monumental ruins which attest the existence of each. The Arkite memorials of circular stone temples, cromlechs, and rocking-stones, are remains of the Cimbrian Druids; while the quadrangular stone temples, the inaugurating, and other circles,[1] are fairly claimed by the Drottes or Gothic priests. Nor does it appear that the votaries of Odin, or their leader, who had assumed the name of the God, although they introduced some civilization, are quite free from the imputation of employing the abominable rites of human sacrifice, performed in the north by the cruel mode of crushing or breaking the spine.

The priests of these barbarous divinities were called Drottr, a name somewhat resembling Druids. They had also the appellations of sages, prophets, and diviners.[2] The priesthood was hereditary in some families, who, like the Incas of Peru, pretended to be the descendants of the Gods.[3] Women being held more particularly sacred, were joined in the sacerdotal functions. These did not scruple to abuse the delicacy of their nature, and imbrue their tender hands in the gore of human victims, pretending to foretel the future by the flowing of their blood,[4] and the appearance of their intestines. White, the emblem of purity, was nevertheless the colour of their garments; avoiding, as they did, the garb of the evil genii and the vulgar, who wore black,[5] as probably, having undergone the diluvian rite of being washed in the waters of the fountain of oblivion.[6]

Such an inspired female was called Fola, and seemed to have been known by that or a similar name among many other nations. Thus Horace, speaking of the Sibylla Ariminensis, calls her Folia,[7] and Tacitus names the celebrated prophetess of the Bructeri, Velleda. The most ancient poem of the Edda is said to be the composition of Vola, Voluspa signifying "inspired speeches."[8]

This plate represents the priest and priestess of the Gothic Scandinavians. His habit is long, his temples are shaved, and the hair on the top of his head hangs down like the Irish glibb, or the tail of the modern Gellong, or Calmuc priest in Russia; and as a distinction from the mere warrior, his beard is unshorn. In his hands he holds a large horn of gold, destined to receive the blood of a human victim. He is attended by a priestess, or Fola, prepared to perform a sacrifice. She holds the knife, inscribed with Rhunic characters, in her hand; her grey hair

C.H.S. del.ʳ   Aquatinted by R. Havell.

A Drotte and a *Folap*.

is unveiled, her bosom is covered by a kind of scapular, and her hips by a piece of linen extremely short. On her legs she wears trowsers like the men; and it is probable that the mantle, similar to that worn by the ancient Irish females, is laid aside for the more convenient performance of her sacred duties.[9]

In the distance is represented a human sacrifice, with the Drottr standing by, the figures being within a parallelogram of stones, which surrounds a barrow, and is still visible on the road to Roskild in Denmark. In the instance given, the female seems to be entirely naked. The whole was copied from the figures engraved on the golden horns found at Galhuus, where the females are seen in the attitude of that in the back ground. The sacrificing knife has been taken from one in the Schachtian Museum at Copenhagen; and a representation of one of the horns of gold, upon which the figures are engraved, has been substituted in the hands of the priest, for the plain one.

Below is a figure of Trigla, the Scandinavian triune deity. Of her three heads, the central is that of Frigga; the right where the hand holds an axe, accompanied by an ear of corn or pointed club, represents Thor, and that on the left, near which is something like a horse, Odin. It is to be remarked that this figure has the appearance of two stars on its body; that on the right breast being larger than the other, and consisting of eight points, while the left one has only six. If the one refers to the sun, and the other to the moon, we have in this compound divinity, the helio-arkite and lunar-arkite deities. Several of the warriors or heroes on the same horn have similar ornaments; and that on the shield invariably corresponds with the one on the breast. The sculptor has marked Trigla of the female sex,[10] though the Gothic divinities, and even the Alsacian Mercury, were often destitute of the sexual character.[11]

[1]Those consisting of thirteen stones in Norway, which seem to mark a lunar year, and the circle of stones near Upsal are of this kind. The Danes erected quadrangular stone temples in Ireland. Suhm, in his observations on Saxo Grammaticus, has the following passage: "It was not difficult for Odin to make the progress which he did in the North; for he gave out that he and his companions were the very Gods who were already worshipped there." That is, the priests of the Asi found so great a similitude between their theology and that of the Cimbri, that they declared their Gods the same. These were consequently the Helio-arkite and Lunar-arkite deities.

[2]As was also the case with the Druids. Mallet's Introd. to Hist. of Denmark, ch. 7.

[3]Diod. Sicul. lib. II. c. 47.

[4]Mallet's Introd. Strabo alludes to a similar custom when he speaks of the pirests of the Cimbri, "Eorum uxoribus in militandi societate conjunctis, consequentes nonnullæ divinationes peritæ sacerdotes adherebant quibus canus capillus erat, alba vestis limtea – aliæ desecto ventre ex intestinis victoriam interpretabantur."

[5]The 8th Triad has the following coincident account. "The third oppression was that of the Cæsarians, who harassed the island for more than 400 years, till their return to Rome to oppose the irruption of the *black horde*;" and the Welsh chronicle generally speaks of the Danes by the name of the black army. The shepherdess Aflauga, wife of Regner Lodbroc, wore a black coarse garment.

[6]The sacret waters of this fountain were white and every thing they touched became as white as the membrane in the inside of an egg. Edda. The Egg was an Arkite symbol.

[7]Epod. v. v. 42.

[8]Mallet, vol. II. p. 267. Edit. Geneve. Fol, in Gothic, has the same signification as in French or English, viz. a person deprived of ordinary reason, by extravagant fanatic delirium, or otherwise.

[9]See Pontoppidan Danske Atlass, vol. I. The Icelandic song of Thrym gives us some female attire. Thus it is said of Freya:

> "Her great bright necklace started wide." v. 49. And again,
> "Now busk we Thor as a bride so fair v. 58.
> "Let him that great bright necklace wear.
> "Round him let ring the spousal keys,
> "And a maiden kyrtle hang to his knees;
> "and on his bosom jewels rare,
> "And high and quaintly braid his hair.
> "He (Thyrm) stooped beneath her veil to kiss.
> "——————— the giant's sister came v. 115.
> "Who dared the bridal gift to claim
> "Those rings of gold from thee I crave, &c.
> "Instead of money and rings I wot" ——— v. 130.

The comparison of this female disguise of Thor, with the descriptions of costume in the Rigs-mal before quoted, gives a clear view of the habits of the Scandinavian females, and proves that even in the tenth century their kyrtles were extremely short. In some parts of Norway, they do not reach much below the knee at this day; and the black colour, bordered with red, is still fashionable among the peasantry.

[10]Mr. Maurice, in the fifth volume of his Indian Antiquities, speaking of the triple deity of the Scandinavians, says that Odin or Woden is the same as Taut, Hermes, and Boodh, Frigga or Freya no other than the Dea Syria adored at Babylon, the Venus Urania of the Persians, and Rhea of the Greeks, while Thor is the Taranis (Pendaran) of the Cimbri, the Eendra of the Indians, and Jupiter Tonans of the Greeks and Romans.

[11]See Montfaucon. Ant. Expl. vol. II. p. 416, et sequentia.

COSTUME OF A PAGAN SAXON CHIEF.

The Welsh bard Aneurin has given us, from his own observation, a detailed account of the person and dress of Hengist, and his description coincides, in most particulars, with the figure of an Anglo-Saxon hero, in a MS. in the British Museum. The subject of this plate has therefore been copied from it.[1] The most striking singularity is the four-pointed helmet on his head, being exactly such as the bard attributes to the Saxons.[2] Similar helmets in the ninth century seem to have been worn in France; for the guards of Lothaire, and Charles le Chauve, are represented as having them, and wearing breast-plates exactly like the one before us.[3] This cuirass is evidently an imitation of the Roman Lorica;[4] but according to the Gododins, Hengist wore "scaly mail," and it seems a surcoat of fur.[5] The spear of this chief is broad and heavy[6] and his convex shield armed with a boss. Hengist, we are told, wore his long red-hair flowing down; he was stout in person, and freckled. When unarmed his head was adorned with a wreath of amber-beads, and round his neck was suspended a golden torque. His banner was red, and exhibited "the picture of the white prancing steed," at once the hieroglyphic of his name, and a symbol of the deity he worshipped.[7]

In the distance is a Saxon ship, taken from the same authority. These vessels were single masted, carrying one square sail. They had curved bottoms, and their prows and poops were adorned with the heads and tails of monsters.[8] These were gilt or painted; and at the mast-head was generally seen a raven, which turned like a weather-cock, to shew the direction of the wind. The raven was sacred to Odin, and is perpetually mentioned by the Scalds, and in the Edda.[9]

Below is a helmet, copied from Montfaucon's Monarchie Françoise, vol. I. pl. xxvi.

[1]Bib. Harl. 603. It represents a chief treading on the body of a vanquished enemy, and serves as an illustration of the CIX. Psalm. It is remarkable that the cup he holds resembles the skull of the human head.

[2]"Redder than purple were the blades of the foe, their white-sheathed piercers, and their four-pointed helmets." Gododin 3d. See also Montfaucon, Mon. Fran. vol. I. pl. xxvi.

[3]The seal of Robert Duke of Burgundy has a figure in the same armour. See Montfaucon's Mon. Fran. vol. I. pl. xxxiv.

[4]In the description of the Saxon forces in the pay of Gwrtheyrn, or Vortigern, the following occurs; "Three hundred knights for the mountain chief (Vortigern) arrayed in gilded armour, three loricated bands, with three commanders wearing gold torques, &c." "gold had collected all these for warfare." See Gododin 7th. Taliesin, in the Cedair Teyrn On, apparently describing Aurelius Ambrosius, says, "then clad in a legionary lorica (Lleon lluryg) a sovereign was exalted."

[5]Aneurin calls him "the wearer of scaly mail, who was harnassed, and armed with a piercing weapon, but covered with the skin of a beast." God. 15th.

[6]This was probably owing to the quantity of Iron in Sweden and its vicinity. The 2nd Gododin says he was armed with "a slaughtering pike." Many of the Saxons also, according to the 10th Gododin, were armed with spears and shields, the latter being made of split wood. 8th Gododin.

[7]Hengist signifies a stallion; the name of his brother Horsa, a horse.

Costume of a *Saxon Chief.*

[8]"And monstrous heads adorn their prows of gold." Battle of Hafur's Bay, v. G.

[9]The mythologists of different nations indulged their fancies to a great degree in regard to symbols. What one regarded as auspicious, another looked on as an ill omen, and vice versa. Thus the raven which Noah sent from the ark never returned; the Britons on that account rejected it, while the Danes, regarding it as the proper emblem of colonists, gloried in its display.

GURM GAMLE, KING OF DENMARK, AND A DANISH YOUTH.

Gurm Gamle, or Gormo the Old, was so called because he lived to the age of 115 years. He began his reign, according to Torfæus, in the year 840, and it is asserted that he died in 935. He reunited the different lordships and principalities to the crown, and achieved the conquest of Norway. Having invaded the territories of the Venades (Wenden) a Sarmatian tribe in Mecklenburgh, they had recourse to the assistance of the Saxons, their allies. Henry the Fowler readily joined them, and their united forces defeated, and compelled Gurm and his people to adopt the Christian religion. The original, from which this figure is copied, is a rude bas-relief, representing Gurm with his hands elevated, while his body is entwined in the folds of a serpent (wurm), which may allude both to his name,[1] and adoption of a new religion.[2] There is a Rhunic epitaph by the side of it, and on the other corner a monster enfolded likewise by a serpent or worm.[3] The king is habited in a corslet of leather (wambas) passing over his *rock* or tunic. This wambas was of painted elk or stag-skin, and was a kind of half armour. On his head he wears a crown, or cap of many folds, such as is seen on the coins of some of the ancient Irish and Anglo-Saxon kings, and was most probably composed of rich stuffs.[4] In his hand has been placed the sceptre or hammer of the northern kings, as represented by Peringskiold in his Uplandic monuments at Robe.[5] "The shape of those hammers, in the time of Paganism, was exactly a cross; for when King Hacon sacrificed with the heathens in Norway, and was forced to drink out of the offering cup, he made the Christian sign of the cross before his mouth; but this was interpreted by his heathen subjects as if he had made the sign of the hammer before his mouth, and so made the libation to the god Thor."[6] It was the symbol of authority; for when the people were convened by the king to the public assembly and court of judicature, the hammer of Thor was used for a sign and summons; but when they became Christians, a cross of wood was substituted. It is probable that the custom of sending a cross of wood imbrued in blood to the different clans, as formerly practised by the Highland chieftains in Scotland, had no other origin.[7] The figure of the king reclines upon a stone, on which is a bas-relief representing Odin upon his eight-footed steed Sleipner.[8] Odin is here habited in a Danish costume, the loose rock, with the trowers or broch,[9] the dress of a modern sailor. The hair of the god is long, and resembles that of the priest."[10]

By the side of the king is a young Danish warrior, holding a bipennis. His tunic is adorned with a broad band of embroidery, and he has greaves on his legs. This figure is taken from Mr. Astle's reliquary, engraved in the Vetusta Monumenta.[12]

Beneath is a coin of the Anglo-Saxon king Ethelred, who reigned from A.D. 675 to 709: and another without inscription, found with a great number at Richborough, near Sandwich. This exhibits a figure, holding the Miölner of Odin. Some have two, in others two figures hold one only. Bishop Batteley thinks

[83]

they are French kings, and signs of Christianity; but it is more probable that they designate kings who reigned some over two kingdoms, where the two crosses appear, and others two over one kingdom, bearing one cross only.

[1]As there is no Rhunic W, another consonant was probably used instead.

[2]The serpent was the symbol of regeneration among heathen nations, and also of the Deity, and therefore it would appear, that if his Pagan subjects did not by this represent him as in the care of their divinity, his Christian followers were strongly bigotted to their heathen mysteries.

[3]The epitaph has been read, "King Harald ordered this tomb to be raised in memory of Gurm, his father, and Thyra, his mother. The Emperor Harald has recovered Denmark." On one side of the stone, Allr aug Nurvieg, and on the other, Aug tiniga folk kristno; implying together, "He converted all Norway and its inhabitants to the Christian faith." Harald has embellished this forced conversion.

[4]There is a representation of a cap, with deep folds or ribs, on the head of one of the Merovingian kings. Montfaucon, Mon. Fran. vol. I. pl. xvii.

[5]The original is seven spans long. In the Edda it is distinguished by the epithet Miölner. The song of Thyrm is on the recovery of this hammer. The kings, governors, and ministers, had formerly permission to use the representation of Thor's hammer as an emblem of the power entrusted to them. The Tau, in the hands of the elders and stewards in the Anglo-Saxon MSS. was probably of similar origin.

[6]Herbert's Icelandic Poetry. Song of Thyrm.

[7]Walter Scott's Lady of the Lake, and Henry's History of Great Britain, vol. I.

[8]Edda. The original bas-relief is engraved in Mallet's Introd. à l'Hist. de Dan. By Sleipner the steed, who carried Odhen, i.e. *the possessor of the circle*, inhabitant of the O, or being of eternity, (for the diluvian patriarch was confounded with the deity) is evidently typified the ark, and by his eight legs the Arkite Ogdoad. It is to be observed that they are birds' claws, and a mythological tale in the Illustrations of Northern Antiq. p. 33; which appears to describe the imitation into the mysteries of the Gothic religion, calling its precepts the language of birds, evidently shews that by these claws is represented also the support of the whole by the priesthood.

[9]"Dani usum Teutonicorum imitantes, quem ex longâ cohabítatione corum dicerunt, et vestitura et armatura se cæteris nationibus coapant, et cum olim formam *nautarum* iu vestitu habuissent propter navium consuetudinem, quia maritima inhabitant, nunc solum scarlatico vario griseo, sed etiam purpura et bysso induuntur. Arnold Abbas Lubescencis, v. 11. c. 5.

[10]Thus in the dying song of Asiborn, it appears that young men wore their hair long:

> "Know, gentle mother, know,
> "Thou wilt not comb my *flowing hair*."

[12]The following description of the Danes is given by Ernold Nigellus, in his Eleg. lib. iv.

> "Hi populi porro veteri cognomine *Deni*,
> Ante vocabantur, et vocitantur adhuc
> *Nort* quoque Francisco dieuntur nomine *Manni*
> Veloces, agiles, armigerique nimis.
> Ipse quidem populus late pernotus habetur
> Lintre dapes quærit, incolitatque mare.
> *Pulcher adest facie, vultuque statuque decorus*
> Unde genus Francis adfore fama refert."

C.H.S. delt.

Aquatinted by R. Havell.

Gurm Gamle, King of Denmark, and a *Danish Youth.*

ANGLO-SAXON KING

AND HIS ARMOUR-BEARER EQUIPPED FOR BATTLE.

ANNO 750.

The Pagon Saxons, as described by Sidonius Apollinaris and Paulus Diaconus, were totally destitute of defensive armour, and almost of clothing; confiding in their lofty statures and hardened constitutions, they defied alike the injuries of the weather and the weapons of the enemy. A short tunic was deemed sufficient to resist the former, and a broad shield served to protect them against the latter: a heavy spear and a broad sword were the offensive arms upon which they chiefly depended. The battle-axe was likewise in common use among them; and it is asserted, that the national denomination of Saxons was derived from Se-ax, the name by which this weapon was distinguished.* But after they had penetrated into the dismembered provinces of the Roman empire, and vanquished nations more civilized than themselves, their love of novelty and natural ingenuity, led them to adopt many habits and customs of those among whom they were settled, and whose religion they had recently begun to approve. Their houses, which hitherto had been circular hovels, assumed a square form; and their ships were likewise improved, by imitating the remains of Roman models. The use of trowsers became common; the hood and mantle was introduced, and they even imitated the practice of painting their bodies. Defensive armour became in vogue; their ancestors had fought bare headed, or protected by incommodious square helmets, which hung like boxes about their temples:† they now assumed the conical cap; and in the specimen before us, we have the first instance that can be found in the designs of the Anglo-Saxons, still extant in this kingdom, of defensive armour. The original is meant to depict Abraham, attended by his armour bearer, engaged against the five kings to rescue his brother Lot. The person of the patriarch or chief, is the only one protected by body armour; and the design tends to prove, that in the eighth century, princes alone, among the Saxons, were provided with such an improved safeguard for their bodies. Judging of the rude design from which the drawing is taken, it would appear, that the lorica or cuirass, consists of some strong substance, probably leather, upon which iron rings have been sowed closely together. His head is encircled with a crown, consisting of a band, surmounted by three *fleur de lys.*

This, Mr. Strutt considers as the cininghelme, or king's crown of Verstegan; but it is probable, that the crown and helmet of a chief was not the same; but that the latter partook of something of the shape of those which are

---

* It is singular that the Saxons should have derived their name from this weapon, and the Franks from the Francia, which was another kind of battle-axe; and yet that modern authors should pretend that the axe and bipennis were solely used by the Danes; probably battle-axes were generally used by all the barbarous tribes, until by commixture with more civilized nations, they gradually relinquished this rude weapon; and the Danes being the last of the northern invaders, were also the last to abandon it.

† There are some instances of this kind of helmets in my own collection of drawings, taken from early Anglo-Saxon MSS. Strutt has likewise published the figure of a king, with a quadrangular crown. See Dresses and Halbits, Plate XVII. See also Montfaucon Mon. Française, Plate XXVI, — These square helmets are noticed by the ancient Welsh bards.

Anglo Saxon King   *of the Eighth Century.*

& his armour bearer.   *Equipped for battle.*

750.

visible on the seals of King Edward the Confessor; that is, a coronet imposed upon a skull cap of leather or metal. In the crowd behind the king is seen a banner, such as are often designed in Saxon illuminations: none, however, are distinguished by armorial bearings, although it is asserted that the first invaders bore the resemblance of a horse in their standards. Sigmund Birken, and other modern Saxon genealogists and heralds affirm, that the two chieftains who first landed in Britain, as well as all their Pagan descendants, bore a black horse (the coal black steed of Odin), and that the white horse was assumed after their conversion to Christianity. But whether Hengest and Horsa assumed the representation of this animal in reverence to the steed of Odin, or as the type of their own names;* or whether it was borrowed from the Britons, is not easy to determine: certain it is, that the figure of a horse, or more properly a mare, was stamped upon British coins as early as the reign of Cunobelin; not indeed as an armorial distinction, but as connected with some mystical reference to the archite worship of the Druids.

In the back-ground are several other Anglo-Saxon warriors engaged in action; below, an ancient specimen of a ship.

AUTHORITIES.

The king and armour-bearer from a MS. in the Cotton library at the British Museum, marked Claudius, B.IV. The ship from a drawing, which I consider as the most ancient delineation now remaining: it is copied from an Anglo-Saxon celestial sphere, in a curious MS. in the Harleian Collection B.M. marked 647. The design represents the constellation *Argo*, and must neccessarily have been a copy of one still more ancient.

* Hengst, a stallion. Horsa, Hros, a horse.

ANGLO-SAXON WOMEN.

ANNO 750.

The Anglo-Saxon women were habited with simplicity, convenience, and elegance; a taste which denotes they were as yet far distant from that restless desire of variety, which is ever attendant on an advanced state of civilization, the characteristic of superfluity, and the companion of luxury. They dressed in long loose gowns reaching down to the ground with large sleeves. Notwithstanding the assertion of Verstegan to the contrary, there is little doubt but they wore linen under the gown; though probably dyed of various colours; and the close sleeves observable within those of the gown, may be conjectured to represent that part of the dress, which, even in the earliest ages, seems to have been worn by all the northern nations. The gown in the illuminations is not unfrequently embellished with bands of different colours, or of embroidery about the knees and at the bottom. It does not appear they wore any other covering for their heads than the veil, coverchief, or hood, which falling down upon the forehead, was carefully wrapped round the neck and shoulders. Their shoes were plain, sometimes slit down the middle of the instep, and commonly of a black colour. Over the shoulders often appear a cloak which seems to have had a hole cut in the middle for the purpose of passing the head through. These general habits continued to be worn for several centuries after the period under consideration, and indeed with little alteration but what arose from a more cultivated attention to the embroidery and disposition of colours down to the end of the Saxon æra. In the oldest manuscripts where colours have been employed, green, blue, and light red seem to have been the predominant hues of the clothing, though there are some pink and others violet, but very few perfectly white.

The figure on horseback has besides the gown and under garment a hood and cloak of the description above mentioned. It is worth observing that riding sideways is not so recent a practice as has been asserted; the figure sits however on the off side of the horse. The other is spinning or winding something from a bobbin. The back-ground is ideal.

AUTHORITIES.

Both the riding and sitting figures, and the axe observable under the horse, are copied from an Anglo-Saxon MS. of the eighth century in the Cottonian Library, B.M. marked Claudius, B. IV. The ancient lyre below, from another somewhat posterior in date, marked Tiberius, B.V.

C.H.S del.ᵗ   Etched by I.A.Atkinson   Aquatinted by Hill

Anglo Saxon Women   *of the VIII Century.*

750

AN ANGLO-SAXON LADY.

ANNO 850.

The plate represents a lady of rank in full dress. On the head she wears a double veil, and a perforated mantle over the shoulders. It is asserted in the most early historians, that the Anglo-Saxon women were celebrated, long before the conquest, for their skill in embroidery; accordingly we find her gown embellished with a border of needle-work edged with beads. The sleeves descend only as far as the elbows, and are of considerable width. Below is seen an under garment with close sleeves, and reaching down to the ground.

Behind the lady appears a kind of vehicle, several specimens of which are to be found in the drawings of that period. The carriage has uprights fixed before and behind with a body shaped like a hammock suspended between. The whole, and in particular the spokes of the wheels, are painted with various colours.

Under the figure are represented a bracelet and signet-ring. Bracelets and rings were worn by both sexes; but the signet-ring was reserved for the great, or men in authority. The place where it was usually fixed is not mentioned. As for the common ring, Mr. Strutt thinks the third finger of the left hand to have been its proper place.

AUTHORITIES.

Lady from an Anglo-Saxon manuscript in the Harleian library, B.M. 2908. Chariot from the Cotton library, marked Claudius, B. IV. Signet and bracelet from Tiberius, C. VI.

C.H.S.del.

Aquatinted by Hill

Etched by I.A.Atkinson

Anglo Saxon Lady

of the IX Century

A.D. 850.

Pub.ᵈ Oct.ʳ 1.1812, by Colnaghi & Cº 23, Cockspur Street, London.

A CAMBRIAN PRINCE,

PRESUMED TO REPRESENT HYWEL DDA, OR HYWEL THE GOOD, KING

OF WALES.

ABOUT THE YEAR 940.

A drawing copied from an ancient Welsh MS. containing the laws of Hywel dda, has furnished us with the curious design, which we conjecture to represent that prince, as he appeared in the hall of judgment. The design, which is necessarily prefixed to the laws, and which contains the figure before us, was copied from the original, as it is intended to represent the disposition of a court of justice, and points out the places where the king and his advisers, the plaintiff and defendant, with their several counsel or friends are to be placed. If it be objected that the costumes of the attendants are more modern than the tenth century, it may be answered that the transcribers might perhaps take that liberty in later copies, as far as it regarded the parties in court, without, on that account, changing the representation of a revered sovereign and legislator.* This opinion is strengthened from the circumstance, that the costume of Hywel is certainly not Anglo-Norman. The crown is rather Anglo-Saxon, and the robe, which he might have brought from Rome, is not of the form worn after the Conquest, but appears to resemble the dalmatics with wide sleeves, observable on ecclesiastical figures designed in the earlier Italian MS. The original is drawn with different coloured inks, so as to convey the idea of a purple robe, lined with ermine and partially bordered with lace. In the Plate before us, the accessories have been omitted, and the King is represented, as entering the porch of his wooden palace on the Tâf,† which, it is fair to conjecture, must have borne something of the character of the wooden church at Greensted in Essex. Hywel went to Rome, on his first journey, in 926, and died anno 948.

AUTHORITIES.

The figure of the King from a drawing copied by Samuel Rush Meyrick, LL.D. and F.A.S. from an original MS. formerly belonging to Sir John Sebright. The building part of the south view of Greensted Church, Essex. Under the figure the representation of an ancient harp, copied from the celebrated harp of the Irish King Brien Boromh, which was carried to Rome in the beginning of the eleventh century, and sent as a present to King Henry VIII. in the sixteenth, and is now in the Museum of Trinity College, Dublin.

* He was only the compiler and midifier of the laws. They were originally edited by Dynnwal Moclmud.

† It was called Ty gwyn ar Dâv, or the White House on the Tâf. See Donovan's Tour in South Wales.

C.H.S.del.ᵗ   Etched by I.A. Atkinson   Aquatinted by Hill

Costume of a   *Cambrian Prince*
presumed to represent Hywel dda   *or Hywel the good*
King of   *Wales.*

ANNO 940.

KING EDGAR, AND A YOUTH OF DISTINCTION.

ANNO 966.

This Costume is taken from an ancient illumination at the head of a book of Grants bestowed by King Edgar himself upon Winchester Cathedral, and dated anno Domini 966. The King is represented in the same attitude as in the original, excepting that both hands are lifted up to heaven; he wears on his head a plain crown of gold; his tunic of purple is short, and discovers the knees bare, at least in the present state of the colouring of the original, the hose are not visible; the leg bandages are of a brown colour, and continue from the calf by a single turn to wind above the knee, where most probably they are fastened to the drawers: the mantle is blue, trimmed in and out side with a broad gold lace, and fastened on the left shoulder by a plain gold fibula. The King holds in his right hand a staff or sceptre of a whimsical form.

By the side of the King is represented an Anglo-Saxon youth of distinction; his mantle fastened on the left shoulder (perhaps as a sign of nobility); the tunic short, and embroidered with various colours; the legs cross-gartered. Both the figures remind the observer of the Highland dress of the present time, and convey an additional proof of its high antiquity. This youth, as well as almost all the figures in Anglo-Saxon illuminations, is represented bare-headed.

In the back-ground is Croyland Bridge, divested of surrounding buildings. Although it is a matter of dispute, whether the present triangular bridge actually stood so early as the tenth century, it is nevertheless certain that the triangular bridge is mentioned in Saxon manuscripts of that period.*

AUTHORITIES.

King Edgar from a Saxon manuscript in golden letters in the Cottonian library, British Museum, marked Vespasianus, A. VIII.; the sceptre or staff from Tiberius, C. VI.

Saxon Youth. Tiberius, C. VI.

Croyland Bridge as it now stands, omitting the buildings.

Implements of husbandry. Julius, A. VI.

*The first mention of this bridge is in the charter of Edred, King of Britain, 943, where the boundaries of Croyland Abbey are thus described:
      "A ponte de Croyland triangulo per aquam de Welland versus
      "Spaldelyng &c."
This passage plainly proves the bridge to be a religious boundary, known as early as 943, and probably built some years sooner. It is conjectured to have been erected by the Abbot some time in the reign of Ethelred, who reigned only from 856 to 860; and this opinion is strengthened by the antique statue of that King being placed upon the bridge. Gough's History of Croyland Abbey, Bib: Top: Brit: vol.III.

King Edgar with an Anglo  *Saxon Youth of distinction.*

966

HABIT OF A BISHOP AND MONK OF THE TENTH CENTURY

ANNO 950.

The art of illuminating books does not seem to have been generally practised until the beginning of the eleventh century. Before that period these embellishments usually consisted of outline drawings done with a pen in different coloured inks. The design from whence the present costume is copied, has been executed in this manner with the addition of a few slight touches of the pencil with colour: it is placed at the head of an Anglo-Saxon translation interlining a Latin paraphrase of the psalms by St. Jerome. The bishop is slightly turned, so as to be viewed a little more sideways than in the original. In his right hand, he holds a maniple, while the other is extended in an attitude of exhortation. His surplice and albe are richly embroidered with flowers, &c. and the whole costume, with the exception of the colours, which vary in all the drawings, and the absence of the mitre and crosier, is similar to that of other prelates and dignified clergymen of the same period. To supply this deficiency, these insignia are displayed below, under the figure, from other documents. Behind the bishop is seen a monk, holding a sacred banner or labarum, such, as, in all probability, was borne before some of the Anglo-Saxon kings, and first preachers of the gospel.* Both stand on the steps of a building with a Saxon archway richly carved in the style of the tenth century.

AUTHORITIES.

The Bishop from an Anglo-Saxon manuscript in the British Museum marked Cotton: Tiberius, C. VI. written in the tenth century. The monk, banner, crosier, book, and mitre from Cotton: Nero, C. IV. The archway from the doorway in Tidmarsh Church, Berks, coloured in imitation of the arch over the original design in Cotton: Tiberius, C. VI.

*For this practice we have the authority of Bede, who reports St. Austin to have had a banner of this kind borne before him during his apostolic labours in this kingdom. *Ecc. Hist. Lib. I. Cap. 25.*

C.H.S. del.   Etched by I.A.Atkinson   Aquatinted by J.Hill

Habit of a Bishop *of the 10.ᵗʰ Century*

950

ANGLO-SAXON MILITARY CHIEF, TRUMPETER, AND WARRIORS.

ANNO 975.

The first Saxon invaders of Britain appeared in the field with little or no defence about their persons, save only what was to be found in hearts the most undaunted, and in a strength of sinews the most firm. They rushed into battle protected by a shield only, bare-headed, and with the sword and spear decided the contest hand to hand with the enemy. But after they had imbibed some dregs of the arts which the Romans had left behind, and the possession of a more genial soil had somewhat softened their martial spirit, they began to assume both breast-plates and helmets. The later species of armour, are of the hauberk kind, ringed, scaly, or of mail: closely resembling those of the earliest Anglo-Normans, though of ruder workmanship, and covering the trunk only. It is now impossible to ascertain positively of what materials the two former, as well as the first helmets, were composed. From the various colours with which they are painted, and the general appearance of their forms, we conjecture them to have been made of the dried or untanned hides of the buffalo and the elk. The shields probably of similar materials, are commonly of an oval shape, stained in circles with different colours round their bosses, and of dimensions so as to cover the body from the chin to the groin. The helmets or caps sometimes indicated the appearance of fur, though more generally that of leather, and in latter times of metal; they are of the Phrygian form, conical, or with serrated crests, and painted with various colours. The spears having long staves, are headed with broad lanceolated or barbed points; and the swords, not as Verstegan asserts, curved, but broad, straight, and of considerable length.

The Chieftain, whose figure we exhibit, has no breast-plate, but an embroidered tunic, and buskins or hose over his trowsers; his helmet and shield seem to be of painted leather, with metal rings round the edges. On his forehead appears the earliest indication of the nasal projection. His sword is ornamented with studs; his spear is barbed; and if the width of the plate would permit, ought to be of sufficient length to poise regularly in his fingers. It has been remarked that there is little projectile power in the manner of his holding this weapon: to this we have no other answer to make than that we have copied the grasp such as it is in the original.

Behind the Warrior is seen a Trumpeter sounding the war trumpet, which seems to be a kind of bugle or buffalo's horn. In the back-ground are Anglo-Saxons charging on horse-back.

AUTHORITIES.

From the Cottonian Collection in the B.M. Chief, Tiberius B.V. Trumpeter, Cleopatra, B. VIII. King and figure with conical cap, Claudius, B. IV. Phrygian cap before the King, Cleopatra, C. VIII.

Arms. A selection of military implements from the authorities just quoted.

C.H.S.del.t

Etched by I.A.Atkinson

Aquatinted by J.Havell

Anglo Saxon Military Chief,   *Trumpeter and Warriors*

97⁵

ANGLO-DANISH WARRIORS.

OF THE REIGN OF KING CNUTE.

ANNO 1035.

From the beginning of the eleventh century, the Danes were greatly intermixed with the Anglo-Saxons. The nobility, in particular, had from the first invasions successfully exerted their valour, characteristic craft, and ambition, to obtain great possessions and influence in the kingdom. These circumstances, and the vicinity of their mutual origin, account for a similarity of manners and customs observable in the two nations. Both were armed with broad-headed spears, and straight ponderous swords: both bore large oval shields, and the bipennis or double axe, by authors usually considered as exclusively a Danish weapon, was sometimes wielded by the hands of Saxons. As a warlike instrument, the bow seems to have been greatly, if not altogether, neglected by this latter people; for if the Bayeux tapestry can be deemed evidence, the small retinue of archers in the train of Harold, proves that his warriors had no reliance on this weapon. With the former, however, the case was in all probability different; for as it is well known that the Normans first introduced the bow into France, there is little doubt, but the Danes (a kindred tribe) imported it into England: nay, the archers with Harold's army, depicted in the above-mentioned tapestry, are probably intended to represent some few Northumbrian settlers, whom his victory in the north had humbled into submission, and the momentary ascendant of the Saxon power had reluctantly forced into his service. In their earlier habits, the Danes are represented with bare heads, and clothed in short tunics; which in process of time, are embellished with broad collars, and borders of embroidery. Mr. Strutt has remarked greaves upon the legs of three Danish figures, carved, and chased in gold, in the possession of Thomas Astle, Esq. Both nations certainly wore hose and shoes. Of the hair they were particularly careful; but the Danes carried their attention to such excess, that they were considered the beaux of the eleventh century.

The plate represents their armour as worn at the close of their dominion in England. The original is executed in colour, with care and splendour; whether the crossed lines delineate scales of metal, or, like the ancient Sarmatians, of horn, sewed on a garment; or whether they be, as Mr. Strutt imagines, wires interwoven with each other, and crossing upon leather; or merely stitches of quilting, containing within scales or rings of metal. Their helmets are more spherical than those of the Anglo-Saxons, and being provided with a substantial nasal, are well adapted to resist the most violent blow from a sword or axe.

Below is a lunated shield or pelta, the peculiar protection of such as bore a bipennis.

AUTHORITIES.

The warriors from an Anglo-Danish MS. prayer-book, said to have been the property of King Cnute the Great, now in the Cotton Library B.M. marked Caligula, A.7. The shield and axe in various illuminations in the B.M.

Anglo-Danish Warriors
of the reign of King Cnute
Etched by I.A.Atkinson
A.D. 1035.

SHIPPING AT THE TIME OF THE CONQUEST.

ANNO 1066.

The Norman nation manifested an early taste for the sea. Already, before the conquest of England, the Ocean and Mediterranean had witnessed its daring valour in naval enterprize. The last of the migratory tribes from the north, it was also the last to retain its courage and pristine institutions. They established their power in Sicily and Naples, in spite of the jealous strength of the Emperors of the East, and the no less jealous ambition of the Popes. In this manner also they were settled in the west of Gaul, although hemmed in by the warlike Franks, and faced by the sea covered with Saxons and Danes.

The questionable succession of Edward the Confessor, had no sooner terminated in the hasty assumption of his Crown by Harold, than William of Normandy determined to assert his pretensions by force of arms. Accordingly, in less than six months he collected a fleet of eight hundred and ninety-six, or as the *Roman du Rou*, cited by Lancelot, affirms, with greater probability, of six hundred and ninety-six vessels: with this fleet, after some delays he crossed the Channel, and landing near Pevensey an army computed at sixty thousand men, he gained in a few days the battle of Hastings, and soon after subdued the whole kingdom. Reflecting on the short space of time allowed for the preparations, and the magnitude of the force assembled for this great undertaking, we cannot refuse our wonder at the resources of the Norman dominions, and admiration of the energy of the government. Allowing these vessels on an average to have carried about an hundred men, the number of builders to construct, and of mariners and rowers to navigate them (even with the admission that many ships and crews were hired), must have been very great.

The subject of the plate before us is taken from the celebrated tapestry of Bayeux, certainly executed soon after the Conquest. It represents, in a series of rude delineations divided into compartments, all the circumstances of that memorable event. The naval compartments are, the landing of Harold on an embassy to the Duke of Normandy; the building of the invader's fleet; is sailing, and arrival. Out of this latter compartment we have selected the Commander's ship, and a horse transport: the other vessel in the distance is taken from an anterior part of the same subject – the departure of Harold for France. Ship-building had in the eleventh century acquired some improvements; there were, at least in the Mediterranean, ships of war with three masts, termed Buccæ. Carricks or hulks were vessels of burthen, by the Latin authors named *naves onerariæ*. Galleys and galiones were of different sorts and dimensions; the former were managed solely by oars; the latter had both oars and a mast and sail: these often carried sixty men in armour, with one hundred and four rowers, besides sailors. Of this class no doubt was the celebrated galley presented by Earl Godwin to Hardi Canute; and the vessel in the centre of the plate is most probably meant to delineate one of the same order. The construction of her hull is considerably curved at the keel, with the stem and stern much elevated; something like modern gondolas, or like Norway fishing-boats: although no indication of oars is to be

C.H.S. delt.

Etched by J.A.Atkinson.

Aquatinted by Merigot.

Ships of William the Conqueror.
A.D. 1066

found, we have no doubt of her capacity to row as well as sail. The rudder is not fixed to the stern-post, but on the quarter, in the manner of the Roman ships, and is paddle-formed, fastened about half way by a chain and bolt. She has but one mast, surmounted by a cross, under which is to be seen the great lantern to conduct the fleet by night, or perhaps a kind of round top for the pilot or sailing captain: the mast is sustained by three pair of stays or ropes, one to the stem, another to the stern, and two to each side. The large square sail is embroidered, and painted near the yard, and most likely altogether of some lively colour, so as to be distinguished at a distance. This sail constantly remained aloft, and when required to be furled, men climbed the mast for that purpose. The steersman holds the helm, and a superior officer sits in the bow. The shields around the gunwale denote her to be equipped for immediate fighting. They are ornamented with various crosses and devices, which, although they are not on the originals, are nevertheless copied from other shields in the same tapestry, and are merely exhibited to show that the Norman shields in those days were already embellished with crosses, monsters, and other symbols.

AUTHORITIES.

The Bayeux Tapestry.

[This is on display in the Musée Tapisserie de la Reine Mathilde in the town of Bayeux in France. It is not a tapestry, but a strip of linen 75 yards long and 20 inches deep embroidered in coloured wool. It is a pictorial account of the Norman Conquest of England showing the clothes mainly of men of different classes and occupations and illustrating the life of the time. The embroidery was worked between October 14th 1066 and July 14th 1077, and it remains the finest source for eleventh-century costume in north-west Europe.]

RICHARD CŒUR DE LION.

ANNO 1189.

The annexed plate represents the Hero of the Crusades, distinguished by the appellation of Cœur de Lion. His great actions are too well known, to warrant in this place any account of his life. It will be sufficient to state that the Costume is taken from the first of the two great seals which he caused to be made during his reign. The drawing is copied from the compared representations in Sandford's Genealogical History, and Dallaway's Inquiry. The King wears on his head a helmet of an eliptical form, bound about the jaws and neck by a flexible substance like cloth, much in the manner of the skull-caps of the modern Mamalukes. The whole body and legs are covered with a hauberk and greaves of scale armour. His right hand sustains a long and ponderous sword, his left a shield embellished with two* lions combatant, and in the middle a boss or projecting point. On the heels he has prick spurs, and his horse's accoutrements are considerably ornamented.

The second seal, which King Richard caused to be made on his return to England after his captivity in Germany, represents him on horseback, habited much in the same manner as in the former, with the exception of the helmet and shield. The shape of the helmet is of the flat kind, ornamented on the top with a crown of what Sandford calls the planta genista; but in the representations of the same seal in Speed and Dallaway, there is, instead, an indistinct stroke like a feather. The visor is a perpendicular plate entirely covering the face, with the exception of three horizontal perforations for the sight and breath, presenting altogether a most hideous appearance. The shield offers the first positive proof of the three lions passant guardant in pale being borne by the Kings of England.

It is worth observing that none of the great seals of the English monarchs, down to the second seal of Richard inclusive, represent the figures on horseback with a surcoat of arms; although the seal of John, used by him before his elevation to the throne, and most likely during his brother's expedition to the Holy Land, bears the impress of his figure adorned with that dress and the nasal helmet. Hence we may perhaps conclude, that the custom originated with the Crusaders both for the purpose of distinguishing the many different nations serving under the banners of the cross, and to throw a veil over the iron armour, so apt to heat excessively when exposed to the direct rays of the sun.

Arms. The shield of St. George, the distinguishing cross of the English during all the Crusades, and borne in the national ensigns to this day; the helmet above the shield is taken from the second seal of King Richard described above. Behind is a sprig of the planta genista, or broom pod, and on the side a battle axe, copied from one kept in the Belfort Tower at Ghent, said to have belonged to Baldwin *bras de fer*, Earl of Flanders, and weighing about eighteen pounds.

AUTHORITIES.

The two great seals of King Richard I. *Vide Speed, Sandford, Dallaway.*

---

*Although on the seal only one of the lions is visible, it is fair to conclude, from the boss or point being on the left of the lion, that another is understood to occupy the half of the shield that is not visible.

[107]

Richard 1st King of England and Earl of Anjou

Duke of Normandy & Aquitain surnamed Coeur de Lion.

11 89

SIR HUGH BARDOLFE, or BARDOLPHE.

ANNO 1204.

This Costume is taken from the fine statue carved in oak on the tomb of Sir Hugh Bardolfe, in the north aisle of the chancel at Banham, Norfolk. "It represents a cumbent knight in armour of mail and small plates, like those on the seal of King Edward the Second; a surcoat and round helmet. A large cinquefoil under his left arm bespeaks him to be Sir Hugh Bardolfe, who had a monument here, and died 1204. It was originally painted over, but is now almost bare: from the little paint remaining we may gather that the mail did not cover the head, but at the height of the mouth was laced with a red lace to a light head piece, which has a kind of crest or sharp eminence, running over it from behind forwards. The arms seem to have been covered with narrow laminæ, and these extended themselves quite over the fingers without dividing them. On the legs the mail seems to be formed of small square figures. The sword, which was placed very forward, is now gone: the sword-belt was of a yellow colour, flowered with green and red; the girdle nearly like it. The surcoat, which is little longer than the coat of mail, is divided about four inches below the girdle; it was of a deep brownish crimson flowered with yellow; on the knees are plates which cover the mail of the legs. The spurs were gilt (the necks lost) and buckled on the instep with leathers painted green, red, yellow, and black. The paint is water colour, laid upon a very thick ground of whiting; which in several places, as the mails for instance, is raised into a kind of relievo, so as to be quite rough to the touch. The colour of the lace which fastens the helmet is exceedingly vivid, owing to being laid upon gold."

See a full account of this statue in Gough's Sepul. Mon. vol. I.

The statue is represented in profile, and the likeness preserved; the attitude is altered into that of life, the sword restored.

Sir Hugh Bardolfe is presumed, by Dugdale, to have been a younger son of the first William Bardolfe, who, 22d of Henry II. was amerced at five marks for trespassing on the King's forests; and was sheriff of Cornwall 31st of Henry II.

Sir Hugh was at first employed in a civil capacity at home, during King Richard's voyage to the Holy Land; although he was soon after present at Messina, in Sicily, and one of those who undertook to make peace between his master and King Tancred. He adhered to the party of John, and opposed Will. de Lonchamp, Bishop of Ely, and was included in the Pope's excommunication. He was held in singular esteem by King Richard, and after his death much engaged in the broils of the Barons. He died the 5th of John, without issue.

Back-ground. Castleacre Castle partly restored. This castle, so called from being in a field, was the ancient seat of the Earls of Warren. John, the last Earl of that name, gave this manor and all his lands to King Edward II. Afterwards King Edward III. in the year 1328, granted the above donation to R. Fitz-Allan, Earl of Arundel, the son of Alice, sister and heir to John, the last Earl.

Arms. The arms of Bardolfe, three cinquefoils, were variously tinctured. Edmonson enumerates no less than eight. In the ancient roll of armorial bearings

[109]

of the knights in the camp of Henry III. (see the Antiquarian Repertory, vol. III. p. 94:)

Sir John Bardolfe, *goulis* III cinquefoils *argent*.

Sir Thos. Bardolfe, *or* III cinquefoils *azure*.

Sir Will. Bardolfe, *azure* III cinquefoils *argent*.

On the roll of the siege of Karlaveroc, which took place in 1300, we find among the barons,

Hue Bardolfe de grand maniere.

Riches, hommes preus et courtois

en azure quint feuilles trois

portoit de fin or es mere.

This agrees with the engraved seal of the Baron of that name who opposed the Pope's usurpations, 29th Edward I.

AUTHORITIES.

Sir Hugh Bardolfe from the statue, as stated above.

The Spear from a manuscript in the Cotton library.

Sword restored, and shield added, from monuments of the 13th century.

Castleacre Castle. Buck's Views.

Sir Hugh  *Bardolf.*

1203.

ALBERIC DE VERE, SECOND EARL OF OXFORD,

LORD HIGH CHAMBERLEYN OF ENGLAND,

AND ADELIZIA, (*daughter of Roger Bigot, Earl of Norfolk*) HIS CONSORT

ANNO 1215.

Alberic or Aubrey de Vere, third of the name, was second Earl of Oxford, after the Conquest. In his youth he followed King Richard I. into Normandy; and, from the circumstances of the effigy, which formerly existed on his tomb at Earlscolne priory in Essex, having lain in a cross-legged attitude, there is some probability that he followed his royal master into Palestine. However this may be, his most essential service appears to have consisted in personal endeavours to collect aid, and, exemplary liberality in bestowing large sums for the redemption of his sovereign. In the tenth of John he became sheriff of Essex and Hertforshire; and from the demise of Richard, he was so great a favourite with John, as to be reputed by the nobles in the fourteenth of that king's reign, one of his evil counsellors. He died in the sixteenth of John, 1215, leaving no issue by his wife, Adelizia, daughter of Roger Bigot, Earl of Norfolk.

The Earl appears in a full suit of mail, or possibly of small scales, gorget, hauberk, and stockings. The skull-cap, ornamented with a fillet denoting his rank, consists of scales. The surcoat is remarkably long and flowered. The shield, which in the original was torn off, is restored. The beard on his upper lip may be conjectured to denote his adherence to the King; who, it is asserted, wore a beard, in contempt of the barons.

Lady Oxford wears on her head a coronet consisting of a circle embellished with jewels; and fastened under the chin by a kind of wrapper. Her gown is long, and about the neck adorned with a rich collar. Over the shoulders is thrown a mantle of state.

AUTHORITIES.

Both the Costumes are copied from original drawings of the monuments in my possession converted from recumbent figures into attitudes of life. The designs are without references, and represent the figures almost in profile. Under the feet of the Earl lies a dog, probably an emblem of his fidelity, and at the feet of his wife a boar, the crest of Vere. There is some difference between them and those Mr. Gough has published from drawings in the possession of the Honourable Horace Walpole. First, the sleeves of the Earl are of mail, or something similar, as well as the whole armour, his skull-cap excepted. Second, there is some appearance of flowers on the surcoat. And, third, the mantle of the lady is more distinctly visible. According to Mr. Gough, the originals were of wood, and totally destroyed in 1736.

C.H.S. delt.

Etched by I.A. Atkinson.

Aquatinted by J. Hill.

Roger Bigot — Earl of Norfolk

1213

Alberic de Vere 2.nd Earl
Chamberlain of England

of Oxford. Lord High
and Adelisia his Countess.

A YOUNG NOBLEMAN OF THE REIGN OF HENRY III.

IN SUMMER DRESS.

ANNO 1250.

This figure is in the habit young people wore on riding abroad in the summer season. The head, instead of a hood, is covered with a white coif fastened under the chin, in form not unlike those sometimes represented on antiques. The gown is plain and loose, descending below the knee as far as the calf of the leg. The toes of the boots terminate in points hanging down below the stirrup irons. The youth has his sword girt on the right side, and on his wrist he bears a hawk, the token of his nobility, and the instrument of his pastime.

In the back-ground are seen two other figures of nearly the same period. The first, leading a couple of dogs, is a game-keeper, seemingly intent on tracking his game; the second, standing behind him, is a sportsman shooting with his cross-bow.

AUTHORITIES.

The Nobleman is copied from a MS. book of fables of the thirteenth century in the Royal Library, B.M. marked 19, C.I. and Harleian 1526 and 1527. The two Sportsmen from Le Livre des Histoires, in the Royal Library, marked 20. D.I.

CH.S. del.   Etched by I.A.Atkinson.   Aquatinted by Hawl.

Costume of a Young *Nobleman of the reign*
of King Henry III *in Summer dress*

Robert de Burgh

1250.

HABITS OF LADIES

IN THE REIGN OF KING HENRY III.

ANNO 1250.

The two females, accompanied by a child, are selected from the same MS. which contains the original illumination of the young nobleman riding with a hawk on his hand, represented in a preceding number. They are habited in gowns and mantles. The hair is gathered in a net wrapped round with the coverchief. That of the young girl is etched with rather too much freedom, as, in the original, there seems to be a more decided intention of parting it on both sides of the forehead behind the ears.

AUTHORITY.

The figures from the Harleian MS. before quoted, marked 1526 and 1527.

Habits of Ladies in the reign of *Henry III.*

1250

Etched by I.A.Atkinson

Aquatinted by Hill

C.H.S.del.

Marshall Earl of Pembroke

REIGN OF KING HENRY III.

This assemblage of groups of different characters is thrown into the form of an historical composition, though all the figures, with little variation in their attitudes, have been copied from one MS. It represents the public entry of a lady of distinction; and conveys an idea of the splendour of a reception, such as Henry III. might have given to the beautiful Eleanor, the wife of his son. The lady rides a palfrey, and is shaded from the sun by a canopy borne by four attendants; behind her is a train of damsels followed by minstrels. Knights and squires in full armour attend the king, who comes out of the gate to meet her: the forms of their shields and banners, together with the mode of blazoning their arms, the want of such bearings on their surcoats, though they are already on the trappings of the horses, tend to prove that the fashion of emblazoned surcoats was not generally prevalent in the middle of the thirteenth century.

AUTHORITY.

From a MS already quoted, marked Royal, 20, D.I.

Costume of the reign of King Henry 3: Anno 1250.

SOLDIERS OF THE REIGN OF KING HENRY III.

ANNO 1259.

With the representations of Anglo-Saxon and Anglo-Danish warriors we have given some account of the earliest specimens of arms and armour now to be found represented in ancient illuminations. We have seen a gradual introduction from the simple shield and battle-axe to the more refined hauberk of ring-mail or scales, and the helmets bending by degrees to something like a visor or guard across the face by the interposition of the nasal bar. When the Normans invaded Britain, and established themselves in their conquest, all the improvements in the art of war, which were known on the continent of Europe, were introduced by them, and defensive armour underwent a variety of alterations.

The foremost figure seems to represent a squire or man at arms. His armour I take to be the intermediate improvement before solid plates of iron were introduced.* It would appear that he is covered with numerous laminæ of iron secured between a succession of hoops of the same metal. On his head he wears a bacinet, which was the usual covering of warriors until they put on the helmet.

By his side stands a cross-bowman, covered with a rude hauberk, and wearing on his head a conical helmet with a nasal. Besides his bow, a cultellum is slung over his shoulder. These cross-bows were in great esteem in England from the reign of Richard I. It was by a wound from this weapon that the warlike Richard fell, and its estimation remained unrivalled until the English bow established its superiority in the reign of Edward III.

Behind them stands an armed peasant, or foot soldier. The diminutive size of his shield is remarkable. The hood on his head and shoulders has the long tail observable in the fashions of the reign of King John.

AUTHORITIES.

Man at arms from a MS. in the Royal Library, B.M., marked Claudius D.II. Spearman, or foot soldier, from a transcript of Matthew Paris in the Cotton Collection, B.M., marked Nero D.I.; cross-bow from another Matthew Paris in Bennet College Library, Cambridge. Both these MSS. bear the evidence of being of the age of the author, and, as he was likewise a painter, we have dated the plate 1259, the year of his death.

---

* There was, however, another kind of mail in use before the plate armour was adopted: it was the double-ring mail, and was probably introduced from the East. This kind of armour lasted from the latter part of the reign of Henry III. to the beginning of Edward III. in the fourteenth century. It was gradually covered by greaves, vambraces, gonfanons and knee-pieces. The oldest specimen of plate-armour I have found is on the seal of Baldwin, Earl of Flanders and Emperor of Constantinople.

Soldiers of the Henry

Monfort of Leicester

1259

Reign of King the third.

AVELINA, COUNTESS OF LANCASTER.

ANNO 1269.

The costume of this celebrated beauty is taken from the sculptured figure on her tomb in Westminster Abbey, now concealed by a modern monument. Although the sharpness of the chiseling is so far destroyed as to leave but little room for the animated remarks of the late Mr. Gough, on the opportunity of engraving this fine statue, reserved for Mr. Bazire; still there is enough remaining to bear testimony of its original beauty; and the Plate by that elegant Artist, proves with what care and taste he handled his subject. The idea of the colouring of the robes is taken from scrapings made with a pen-knife from some of the least exposed parts of the drapery, and the design of the patterns from an illumination executed about the period in question. The head is attired in a veil, or perhaps more properly in a wimple and gorget, with *bindæ* (a kind of riband) on the forehead. The gown under the surcoat or super-tunic is visible only by the extremity of the sleeves reaching beyond the other, and over the shoulders is thrown the mantle. Behind the Countess are seen two young females of the same period, habited in gowns and super-tunics, shewing the gorgets without veils or wimples.

Avelina was the first wife of Edmund Crouchback, Earl of Lancaster, and daughter and heir of William de Fortibus, Earl of Albemarle, by Isabel, daughter of Baldwin IV. sister and heir to Baldwin de Ripariis (or Rivers), fifth and last Earl of Devon of that family, married to him in the 53d (according to Sandford) or 54th, if we credit Dugdale, of Henry III. 6th Ides of April, 1269; and, it seems, deceased the same year without issue. She had been united in first wedlock with Ingram de Percy, Lord Dalton, and consequently cannot have been very young at the time of her death.

Back-ground. Part of Lancaster Castle.

AUTHORITIES.

The Figure from the monument in Westminster Abbey. Two Ladies from Brit. Mus. Sloane. 3983.

Lancaster Castle. Buck.

C.H.S. dd.ᵗ

Aquatinted by J. Hill

1269

Avelina, Daughter & heir of William   de Fortibus, Earl of Albemarle,
First Wife of Edmund   Crouchback, Earl of Lancaster.

SHIPPING, VARIOUS COSTUMES, AND BUILDINGS OF THE REIGN OF KING HENRY III.

ANNO 1269.

The different objects grouped together in the plate are selected from a most curious manuscript in the British Museum, entitled *Le Livre des Histoires*; which, as far as the hand writing and the illuminations can be trusted, must be referred to the middle of the 13th century. No other liberty has been taken with the originals, than to place them in the form of a composition, leaving all the particulars in their primitive state, the attitudes of two or three figures excepted. The date* affixed to this description is chosen, with a view to point out the particular period, when shipping, such as represented in the plate, were in use: although that method of constructing was practised both before and after. In all probability, the long sea-voyages performed in the crusades, increased the attention to nautical affairs, and produced material improvements in the building of vessels. In Europe, at least, no ships were constructed capable of bearing a number of horses for a long voyage until the twelfth century. William Archbishop of Tyre, after describing the ships of war, which he denominates galeasses (galeæ) as longer than others, furnished with beaks, and having double banks of oars: continues, "among these were sixty of a larger class, to transport horses, fitted with ports in the poops, which when open served to embark and debark; and with bridges, for the convenience of landing both men and horses."

As the memoirs of the Lord John de Joinville throw some light on this subject and give a lively picture of the manners of the time, we beg leave to subjoin an extract from Mr. Johnes's valuable translation.

Joinville relates his embarkation in the following terms:

"It was in the month of August, in this same year (1245) that we embarked at the rock of Marseilles, and the port of the vessel was opened to allow the horses we intended carrying with us to enter. When we were all on board, the port was calked and stopped up as close as a large tun of wine; because, when the vessel was at sea, the port was under water. Shortly after, the captain of the ship, cried out to his people on its prow, Is your work done? are we ready? they replied, Yes! in truth we are. When the priests and clerks embarked, the captain made them mount to the castle of the ship and chaunt psalms in praise of God, &c. . . . and while they were singing, a breeze filled our sails and soon made us loose sight of land: so that we only saw sea and sky, &c. . . . "

What Joinville calls the castle of the ship is very distinct, and a person is seen standing upon it by the side of the banner-bearer, sounding a war instrument, most probably the nacaire or Saracen trumpet, so often mentioned in the histories of the crusades.

AUTHORITY.

The whole from a MS. in the British Museum marked Royal, 20, D.I.

---

* In the year 1269 the crusade of Edward Longshanks, afterwards Edward I. and his brother Edmund, was undertaken.

[124]

C.H.S. del.

Etched by I.A. Atkinson

Aquatinted by Howitt

Shipping &c. of the reign of King Henry 3rd

Anno 1260.

JESTERS, OR FOOLS.

ANNO 1272.

It is probable that the introduction of jesters or fools, like many other of our early customs, is derived from the East. Hindoos and Mahomedans still continue to revere ideots as the favoured of heaven, and possibly the innovation of substituting knaves for ideots was an improvement of European taste. A real changeling could afford but transient sport to the coarse feelings of semi-barbarians, a jester was, therefore, a more desirable acquisition; and, accordingly, we see, in the progress of civilization, the fool replaced by the jester, and this latter gradually refined, till at length he often proved to be the most sensible personage in the family where he was maintained. Archy, the celebrated humourist, has left his name to a waggish turn of expression, and the last of the profession, in England, has proved, that even a mitre was not insensible to the piercing keenness of his jeers.* But, if, at length, the cap and bells were banished from the court, popular assemblies long retained their relish for them. In my youth, I still remember being shewn, in Flanders, the motly garb and bells of the fool, belonging to a gild or confraternity of archers. The late professor of mirth, among the Flemish boors, had been a cobler, and I was told, that in his day, he appeared the privileged personage of the society, and, that every quirk was repaid with the loud laughter of his broad-faced employers.

The original illumination, from which the figure in the foreground is taken, represents a fool receiving, from a king, a paper, probably a grant of some intended benefit. It is painted in the initial letter, but the page, upon which it is found, is left blank, which proves that the gift was never completed. From the style of painting, it must belong to the reign of Henry III.; for Edward I. could hardly be presumed to have squandered his favours on men, whose society so ill fitted the English Justinian. The attitude is slightly altered, in one hand he holds a stick to which an inflated bladder is fastened, in the other a paper or folded parchment. His legs and feet being bare attest that, in the 13th century, the quality of fool had not yet risen into the consideration which it afterwards obtained, under the name of jester. Below is a fool of the 15th century.

AUTHORITIES.

The figure in the foreground is copied, as said above, from an initial letter painted on a blank leaf, and inserted in a book of the Cotton Collection, B.M., marked Nero C.V. – The fool, in the back-ground, from the Harleian, No.2840. – That below, from a MS. copy of Froissart, in the Harleian, No.4380.

* Archy, or Archee Armstrong, jester to James I. and Charles I. &c.; he had his hood pulled over his head, and was dismissed his office, at the instigation of Archbishop Laud for his sarcastic prayer: "Great praise be given to God, and little *Laud* to the devil."

[126]

Fools; or   *Jesters.*

1272

SIR ROGER DE TRUMPINGTON.

ANNO 1289.

The interesting specimen before us is taken from a brass monumental plate representing a cross-legged knight in Trumpington church, in the county of Cambridge. The figure has been commonly ascribed to Sir Giles de Trumpington, who flourished in the reign of King Henry III., and is named in the list of warriors in his camp;* but Mr. Lysons† has referred it to Sir Roger de Trumpington on account of the armour being of a later fashion, and his opinion is the more probable because the Trumpingtons only succeeded the Caillys by marriage in the reign of Edward I.,‡ and Sir Roger died in the seventeenth of that king. The costume is certainly that of the end of the thirteenth and beginning of the fourteenth centuries, and offers one of the most complete representations extant, of the military habit of that warlike period.

The knight is clothed in a suit of mail from head to foot; his knee-pieces only being plate armour. His helmet being of the pointed, conical kind, and without moveable vizor, is fastened by a chain to a cord round his waist. It is destitute of crest, and in front ornamented with a cross flory, through the horizontal bar of which apertures are made, to permit the wearer to see. His shield, decorated with the arms of Trumpington, is triangular and much curved. The gonfanons behind his shoulders, and the scabbard of his sword, are likewise embellished with his family arms, differenced with labels of five points. His sword, broad and massy, is buckled forward upon the thigh, and his heels are armed with a pair of large prick spurs. His surcoat is long, and without ornaments or emblazoned distinctions.

The whole of this costume coincides exactly with the period above stated; for gonfanons did not come into use till the close of the thirteenth century, and were laid aside about the middle of the reign of Edward III. The shape of the sword, and mode of buckling it on, the size and form of the shield, together with the spurs, all indicate the costume of the reign of King Edward I.

Arms. Azure, crusule two trumpets in pale *or*, Trumpington.

AUTHORITY.

From a drawing of the monumental plate in Trumpington church, county of Cambridge.

* See Antiquarian Repertory, Vol. III. p. 94. Cambridge.
† Lysons's Britannia, Vol. II. page 65.
‡ Gough Vol. I. p. 219.

Sir Roger de *Trumpington.*

1289.

A SCOTS KNIGHT,

SUPPOSED TO REPRESENT THE PERSON OF A CHIEF OF THE ISLES,
TEMPORE EDW. I. ET ROBERTI DE BRUCE.

ANNO 1306.

Although the person represented by the figure cannot be identified, nor the time to which the costume strictly belongs, be ascertained with precision, we have been induced to give it a place in this work, on account of the extreme paucity of satisfactory materials relative to Scotland that have come to our knowledge. The original drawing was communicated by a friend, and is the same as delineated in Mr. Pennant's tour. From the circumstance of the shield bearing a ship with sails trussed up, it may be inferred that he was a chieftain descended from the ancient Kings of Man of the Norwegian race,* a Lord of the Isles, or an Earl of Arran. The lion rampant in the base with something like a tressure around him may denote some connection with the Kings of Scotland.

The costume agrees perfectly with the idea that can be formed of the Scots warriors, before their connections with France, as described by Froissart: he relates that they were very inadequately furnished with defensive armour until Charles VI. sent to their assistance a body of French knights, and a supply of armour which he had obtained by disarming the mutinous Parisians.

The knight is leaning on a spear with a leaf-shaped blade; on his head he wears a small skull-cap, like some of the ancient Anglo-Saxon warriors of the 11th century. He is habited in a surcoat of a kind of cloth, which, on account of the well-authenticated fact that tartan† was in use long before the period in question, we have considered as the most probable substance intended to be here represented: the form of his shield and broadsword fix the time to some period in the reigns above stated. The purse testifies the antiquity of its use, and the whilk or conch shell, which Mr. Pennant seems to have considered as a drinking vessel, is rather a war trumpet worn for the purpose of sounding the gathering call of the clan, and bring them together. In the back ground is the cathedral church of Iona or Ilcolmkill, where the monument is to be found.

AUTHORITY.

From a sketch communicated by Mr. Fraser.

* The ship is a charge frequently seen on the arms of the ancient Scots nobility. The Kings of Man, of the Norwegian race, bore *argent* a ship with sails trussed up *sable*. – The ancient Earls of Arran the same.
† Upon a Roman tile at Cambridge, representing two British prisoners led by Roman soldiers, the tartan clothing is perfectly distinguishable. Strabo and Xiphilin (ex Dion. in Nerone) have also given a very perfect description of the tartan dress worn by Boadicea; Diodorus Siculus and Pliny seem to allude to tartan in their accounts of the dress of the Belgic Gauls. David Earl of Huntingdon, 1120, afterwards King of Scotland, is likewise represented on horseback on his seal in a surcoat to all appearance of tartan.

C.H.S. del.

Etched by I.A. Atkinson

Aquatinted by Havell

A Scots Knight

the person of a

Temp.** Edwardi 1

supposed to represent

chief of the Isles

& Roberti de Bruce.

Old Earls of Arran

1306

A KNIGHT TEMPLAR IN HIS MILITARY HABIT.

ANNO CIRCITER 1309.

The order of the Templars was the first of all the military-religious orders. It was founded at Jerusalem, about the year 1118, by Hugo de Paganes and Jeffery de St. Ademar; who united with seven others for the defence of the Holy Sepulchre and the protection of pilgrims who went thither to perform their devotions. Baldwin II. King of Jerusalem, furnished them with a house, near the church, said formerly to have been the Temple of Solomon. Hence they obtained the name of Templars, or Knights of the militia of the Temple: and it was also owing to this circumstance that their houses were called Temples.

On account of their poverty, the knights were at first denominated the poor of the Holy City; and to announce their humility, they selected for a device on their seal, two men riding one horse. They subsisted on alms, till the King of Jerusalem, the prelates, and grandees, vied with each other in bestowing a multitude of gifts; some for a time only, and others to perpetuity.

The nine original knights, made conjointly the three *vows of religion, poverty, chastity* and *obedience*; to which they added a fourth, which bound them to defend pilgrims, and to keep the high roads safe for such as undertook the pilgrimage to the Holy Land. They admitted no associates until the year 1125, when they received the rule of St. Bernard, after the council of Troyes, in Champagne, by the Bishop of Alba, legate of Pope Honorius II.; this council enjoined they should wear a white habit, and in 1146 Pope Eugenius III. added a red cross to be worn on their caps and mantles. In a short time they became so numerous that in their convent they were more than 300 knights, besides a vast body of brethren. The order was finally extinguished in 1312.

The annexed figure is taken from the print in Dugdale's Monasticon, compared with an early Italian representation. The knight wears the red cap upon his coif,* and the cross on his mantle: his surcoat is also white. It is probable that the professed knights were not permitted to wear any surcoats blazoned with their family arms, but that their distinctive cross was permitted to be worn on the breast in battle, where they appeared of course without mantles: on the back they had none, that the sign of the cross might never be seen to fly. The Templars, in common with the Knights Hospitalers and the Teutonic order, were not permitted to turn their backs upon the enemy. In his right hand he holds a staff similar to those still borne by the modern Circassians: leaded at top and pointed below, it served as a mace, and could likewise be thrown like a dart with considerable force: his armour is of mail; below is the cross which the modern authors on the Orders of Knighthood affirm to have been worn pendent from their necks.

* See William Darrell's description of a Knight Templar, quoted in Dugdale's Warwickshire, page 704.

A Knight Templar  *of the XIV Century*

in his military *habit*

1309

THOMAS, EARL OF LANCASTER, LEICESTER, DERBY,

AND LINCOLN, AND STEWARD OF ENGLAND.

ANNO 1314.

He was the eldest son and heir of Edmund, surnamed Crouchback, Earl of Lancaster, by his second wife Blanche of Artois, Queen of Navarre. The splendour of his birth, and the vast possessions which he held in his own right, and by his marriage with Alice, daughter and heiress of Henry Lacy, Earl of Lincoln, rendered him for a time the most powerful baron in the kingdom. Being of a turbulent disposition, and conscious of his rank and importance, he felt disgusted at the influence which Gaveston and the two Spencers successively exercised over the mind of his sovereign. His resentment kindled into rebellion, and made him instrumental in the death of the former, and banishment of the latter. But while his fortune was impaired by the strange separation from his wife, he ventured a third time to take up arms and to march northward, intending to join some other disaffected and hostile forces. The step was fatal, for being encountered at Boroughbridge by Sir Andrew de Harcla, he was defeated and taken; and a few days after beheaded in his own castle of Pontefract, an. 15 Edward II. 1322.

The figure is copied from his seal, and exhibits one of the earliest instances of an emblazoned surcoat, and the first among the seals of the royal family, bearing a crest and lambrequin or mantling suspended from the helmet. This crest is a weevern or dragon, and is repeated on the horse's head between a pair of straight horns. It seems that the custom of embellishing the caparisons of the horses with the arms of the rider, is anterior to the fashion of wearing emblazoned surcoats, as the seals of the two first Edwards testify.*

AUTHORITY.

The figure and arms from the large seal in the Cotton Library, quoted and figured in Sandford's History; vide page 107.

* The most ancient we have met with is, the seal of Saer de Quincy, first Earl of Winchester. His arms are on the banner, shield and caparisons of the horse. If we refer the making of the seal to the date of his creation, it will be as early as 1207; if to the year of his death, no later than 1219. The first instance of an emblazoned surcoat is in the lives of the two Offias, by the hand of Matthew Paris, which cannot be much earlier than 1250. Those painted on the monumental figures of Robert of Normandy and William Longespec, are, to all appearances, done long after the tombs were constructed.

C.H.S del.

Etched by I.A.Atkinson

Hill sculp.t

Thomas, Earl of Lancaster,   *Leicester, Derby & Lincoln,*

and Steward   *of England.*

1314

A HORSE LITTER.

ANNO 1325.

In the earlier ages, when Europe began to emerge from barbarism, the first care of society was directed towards the acquisition of the necessaries and convenience of life; but when these had attained a certain degree of perfection, luxury and the refinements of elegance soon followed. As every nation was warlike the men universally rode on horseback. Mules were reserved for the clergy, and females were indulged with the occasional use of the litter. Chariots had, indeed, been in use among the Greeks and Romans, but they seem not to have been adapted to the purposes of travelling. The horse litter, being a simple and obvious instrument, may have been the invention of every nation, but as it is still used in China, Persia, Turkey, Sicily, and Spain, it has probably been imported by the Crusaders from the East, and continued in vogue in every country, where the badness of the roads, or the roughness of the soil has rendered the introduction of carriages on springs impracticable.

The vehicle, being of a simple construction, is nearly the same, from the earliest specimens to those of the present times. The materials and finish of the workmanship consituting the only observable difference. That before us, being copied from the earliest specimen which has come to my hands, is more in the form of a couch or palankeen; in later specimens they are deeper, so that the persons within could sit instead of lying down. The latest I have met with, as used by English or French ladies, may be seen in the picture of the *Champ du Drap d'or* in the meeting room of the Antiquarian Society.

AUTHORITY.

From a MS. in the British Museum, Royal, 16, G. VI. *Gestes des Rois de France, jusqu'à la Mort de St. Louis.* This MS. belonged to Humphry Duke of Gloucester. It must have been written and illuminated about a century before it came into his possession.

C.H.S. del.^t

Etch'd by I.I.Atkinson

Aquatinted by Hill

A Horse Litter. Anno 1325.

SIR JOHN DE SITSYLT OR SEISYLT (CECIL), KNIGHT.

ANNO 1333.

The Plate represents a costume such as knights and barons used to assume on appearing within the lists upon solemn occasions. The ample robe of a red colour and lined with ermine denotes the dignity of the wearer to be a knight, and the banner and sheild emblazoned with arms, attest the name of his family. Figures, either whole or half-lengths, holding shields and banners of arms, are occasionally found depicted on heraldic and genealogical compilations of the 13th and 14th centuries. Of this kind is the ancient muster-roll of the knights at the siege of Karlaveroc castle.

The family of Sitsylt or Seisylt (since called Cecil) is descended from Robert ab Seisylt, a Cambrian gentleman, who with other chieftains of his nation, assisted Robert Fitzhamon in the reduction of Glamorganshire; he married a lady, heiress of Alter Ynys and other lands in Herefordshire; by which means he became seated in that county. His son, James de Sitsylt, took part with the Empress Maud against King Stephen, and was slain at the siege of Wallingford, anno 1142, "having then upon him a vesture whereon was wrought in needle-work his arms or ensignes as they be made on the toombe of Gerald Sitsylt in the abbeie of Dorc." Sir John, the eleventh in descent from Robert, was a knight in the reign of King Edward III., and "had a charge of men at arms for the custodie of the marshes of Scotland." He married Alicia, sister to Sir Richard Baskerville, Knt. who had married his sister. In the sixth of Edward III. while the army lay at Halydon Hill near Berwick, a dispute arose between him and William de Faknaham, on the subject of the armorial bearings of both being the same. After the parties had offered to decide the cause by combat, it was finally determined by the judgment of Edward de Beauville and John de Mowbray, in favour of Sitsylt, and the use of similar bearings forbidden to the other. From this family the present Marquisses of Salisbury and Exeter are descended.

Although the original figure from which the Costume is taken, was most probably illuminated by the King's heralds after the dispute above mentioned, and can therefore not be dated before the year 1333; yet the dress belongs more properly to the reign of Edward II. and this may be accounted for by supposing that the illuminators of the patents of arms, designed to represent James de Sitsylt, the fifth of the family proved to have borne the arms in question.

AUTHORITIES.

From a small illumination on vellum, penes me, similar to the figure in Boswell's *Concords of Armorie*. See also Bissæi notæ in Nic. Upton, de studio militare. Londini, 1654.

Etched by I.A. Atkinson

Aquatinted by Hill

John de Mowbray

1333

Sir John   *Titsylt Knight.*

PHILIPPA OF HAINAULT, QUEEN OF ENGLAND.

ANNO 1369.

The effigy of this princess, on her tomb in Westminster Abbey, bears all the characteristic marks of a portrait, and, though the features of the face were probably taken at the time of her death, when she must have been nearly sixty years of age, they exhibit a strong character, a masculine mind blended with uncommon majesty and beauty. It is, unquestionably, the best executed portrait of that age now remaining in the kingdom. The statue was originally painted and adorned with embellishments of extraneous substances. About the head-dress (now greatly mutilated) there are still the remains of iron pins, which probably fastened imitations of pearls on the cowl of network which incloses the hair. The crown is obliterated, and the sceptre, which once was held in her hand, is gone. Her gown is plain, and laced close to the body, with sleeves buttoned tight to the arms and reaching to the middle of the hands: she wears a small belt round the hips, and her mantle is fastened to the shoulders by a simple cord. We have altered this statue to the attitude of life, and restored the mutilations and colouring from illuminated specimens in contemporary MSS.

The life of this great queen is too well known to allow of any detailed account of her actions. In the course of a long and glorious reign, she acquired and preserved the esteem and affection of the English nation. As a wife, as a mother, as a queen, she was the subject of universal admiration; and no circumstance of her career throws so great a lustre over her virtues, as that the great Edward himself could no longer sustain the burthen of his glory when deprived of his illustrious consort.

AUTHORITY.

The effigy on her tomb in Westminster Abbey.

C.H.S. del.ⁿ   Etched by I.A.Atkinson.   Aquatinted by Havell

Philippa *of Hainault,*
Queen of *England*

13 69.

TRUMPETERS PLAYING IN CONCERT.

ANNO 1375.

Musicians performing on different instruments were among the first class of domestics in the houses of the great: their existence may be traced up to the remotest periods of civilization. In this kingdom the British chiefs had bards, and the Saxon kings minstrels; and so essential a part of the household were they reckoned, that even now the race of domestic harpers among the Cambrians, and of pipers among the Scots, can hardly be deemed extinct.

The specimen before us does not exhibit personages of the heroic or nobler class; they are mere performers, and the singularity of their costume tends to prove, that in their habilliments, the love of the grotesque was already discernible, so early as the reign of Edward III.

Below are various instruments of the fourteenth century.

AUTHORITIES.

The figures from Royal, 15, D. III, in the British Museum: being a transcript of *La bible historiaulx, par Pierre Doyen de Troyes, trans. par un chanoine de St. Pierre d'Aire*, A.D. 1291–4: the copy is of the latter end of King Edward III.

The instruments from Royal, 2, B. VII.

Trumpeters *performing in Concert*

1375

SHIPS OF THE FOURTEENTH AND FIFTEENTH CENTURIES.

FROM 1375 TO 1425.

From the inspection of the Plate, it will readily be perceived, that no improvement of moment had taken place, in the construction of shipping, from the times of the crusades, as represented in a former number, down to the period now under consideration. In form, the hulls and lofty extremities remained essentially the same, and it is fair to presume, that, limited as experience in the true principles of naval architecture then was, the warriors (who in those days fought either hand to hand with their enemies, or with missiles of short ranges) derived considerable advantage from being placed on elevated platforms, in shape not unlike the turret-defences on land. That this eminence of station added materially to the security of vessels, we may infer from the frequent mention made in our early historians of Spanish ships being with greater difficulty assailed or captured, because their bulk was larger, and their castles loftier than those of the English.

The vessel in the back-ground with its stern visible, is of the reign of Richard II.; the afterpart is considerably elevated; and on the prow we perceive a tower; besides the main mast, there is a smaller close to the stern.

The ship in front is a man of war (such as King Henry V. employed in his expeditions against France) furnished with three masts and sails, and having, from a lofty forecastle, a spar projecting for a bowsprit. The poop is not quite so high as in anterior specimens, and below are perceivable what may be taken for a row of cabin windows, or round port-holes. From the main top, emblazoned with arms, is seen flying the royal standard, and within it, a quantity of darts ready to be flung at the enemy. The sides of the ship are ornamented with a row of shields bearing the arms of the principal persons embarked. In the original illumination, these armorial bearings cannot be traced to any particular families, if we except a few within the vessel: we have therefore taken the liberty of suppressing them, and substituting the arms of some of the most distinguished characters in the French wars under King Henry V. or of persons known to have been attached to his household.

The distance represents the Isle of Wight, with the Needles and the Hampshire shore.

AUTHORITIES.

The ship with the stern visible, from an illuminated MS. in the Cotton Library, B.M., Domitian, A. 17. The ship in front from a MS. Froissart, illuminated early in the 15th century, in the Harleian Collection, B.M., marked 4379. The arms from different heraldic works.

C.H.S. del.

Etched by I.A.Atkinson.

Aquatinted by Howitt.

Ships of the 14th & 15th Centuries.

ARTILLERY, CROSS-BOW MEN, ARCHERS, &c.

OF THE FOURTEENTH AND FIFTEENTH CENTURIES.

ANNO 1375—1425.

When gunpowder was first discovered to possess a projectile power, its military application was confined to a kind of mortar, or bombard, intended as a substitute for the enormous battering machines then usually constructed. None of the countries of Europe having convenient roads, and all many strong castles, war engines less bulky and more portable were particularly desirable for invading armies: also we find that Edward III. had artillery as early as the middle of the 14th century.* The first guns were made of bars of iron, strengthened with hoops of the same metal, welded together. They were short pieces with large bores, and had usually chambers. The precise purpose for which they were used, was to throw, on the principle of the balistæ, bullets of lead or stone over the walls, to ruin the roofs of houses, the parapets, and other defences of a town; the ranges describing parabolic curves of little more than 300 yards radius.

Both the specimens in the Plate are of the bombard, or mortar kind; that seen in the middle is the oldest delineation we have found among the illuminations in the British Museum. The carriage is slight in proportion to the bulk of the piece. The other, seen in the fore-ground, is of a construction somewhat later: the cannon is of iron, and lies in a kind of trough or bed continued to the earth, not unlike a modern horse artillery trail: the whole resting on a pintle, or moveable pivot, fixed in a strong upright erected on a square timber frame. By the muzzle of one of the guns stands a broad-shield bearer, or paviser: the denomination of subordinate soldiers, whose duty was to bear a large shield before the gunners, archers, and cross-bow men, who approached the walls thus protected. The group in the centre consists of a gunner, an archer, and another cross-bow man. In the back-ground are soldiers, the marshal standing in front with his banner-bearer before him.

AUTHORITIES.

The gun in the middle, gunner, archer, and cross-bow man in the fore-ground, the marshal, banner-bearer, and part of the town from Sloane, 2433. Chronique de St. Denis.

The cross-bow man in mail armour and purple surcoat, is in a costume more frequently observed in illuminations of the reign of Edward III.; he is copied from Royal, 16. G.V. Chronique des Rois de France, a manuscript, once the property of Humphrey Duke of Gloucester.

The gun in the fore-ground, with the paviser, from Harl. 4425, a beautiful copy of the Roman de la Rose of the 15th century.

* Indeed John Barbour, Archdeacon of Aberdeen, in his romance of Robert Bruce, calls guns crakys of war, and reports them to have been used in Edward the Third's army, A.D. 1327; and Vilani asserts he had some at Crecy, 1346.

Artillery, Warlike Machines and Soldiers of the 15ᵗʰ Century

EDWARD THE BLACK PRINCE.

ANNO 1376.

Notwithstanding the lapse of more than four centuries, there are many representations of this great Prince still in existence: of these, the most authentic and interesting, for Costume or Portrait, are, his elegant monumental effigy in Canterbury Cathedral; a mourning figure on the tomb of Edward the Third; three different impresses of his seals; and two illuminations preserved in the British Museum. It will perhaps not be uninteresting to collect in one point of view, a short sketch of these several figures, pointing out the essentials with regard to costume, and the marks of resemblance or difference in each.

Of the Seals, the first in point of antiquity represents the Prince on horseback, clad in mail, with a curious helmet.* His shield, surcoat, gonfanons and horse trappings, adorned with the arms of England singly, and the label of three points over all. His sword appears borne without a scabbard, by a chain of the length of the arm, fastened to the breast, and extending to the pummel. The next Impress exhibits also a figure on horseback; but here the arms are quartered of France and England, and on the helmet is a cap of maintenance surmounted by a lion statant guardant. On the third, which was the Prince's seal, as Duke of Aquitain, he is represented sitting in his robes of state, a wand in the hand, and a fillet round the head. It is remarkable that the face is not bearded.

The mourning figure† is clothed in a long mantle, the face bearing evident resemblance to the statue on his tomb.

On examining the Illuminations, we find him in the first‡ with one knee bended, resting on his cervelliere, and receiving from the hands of his father (who is seated), the grant of the Dutchy of Aquitain; both figures are in plate-armour, with their surcoats properly blazoned; the Prince bare-headed, with a plain gold fillet about the temples, his hair cut round, and a beard on the chin and upper lip. We may remark, that the gorget of mail is in this instance fastened to the cervelliere, or skull-cap. This interesting incident is painted within the initial letter of the deed above alluded to. The other Illumination§ here noticed, exhibits the Prince in long robes of blue, powdered with flowers de luce, and lined with ermine. The head is crowned with a circle of roundels surmounted by trefoils, is bearded, and has sufficient marks of resemblance to the mourning and kneeling figures, to prove that they were all intended for portraits.

But the representation of this hero on the plate is taken from the beautiful effigy of copper on the monument in Canterbury Cathedral. The statue is in plated armour, a pointed skull-cap, adorned with a coronet, a gorget of mail, and a surcoat of arms quartering Old France, and England, under a label of three

---

* See a copy of this helmet in Grose's Treatise on Ancient Armour, Plate IX. fig. 16; also the delineations of the Impresses above mentioned in Sandford's Genealogical History.

† See the tomb of Edward III. in Westminster Abbey. This figure is engraved in Carter.

‡ See British Museum, Cotton. Nero. D. VI. A volume of treatises, charters, &c.; also Strutt's Royal and Ecclesiastical Antiquities.

§ See Cotton, Domitian, A. XVII. copied in Strutt's Dresses and Habits, Plate LXXXIV.

Edward Prince of Aquitain & Wales Duke of Cornwall
& Earl of Chester surnamed of Woodstock

13 76.

points. The hips are encircled by a girdle of lions' heads richly carved. The shoes piqued, and the spurs furnished with large rowels. Taking the proportions of the statue for a close copy of nature, the Prince must have been somewhat above six feet in stature, with limbs finely formed, a countenance indicating languor, a nose well shaped, and a quantity of hair on the upper lip. By his side are his shield and helmet (the latter copied from that under the head on the tomb,) with the ostrich feathers overshadowing the lion, here represented couchant. Behind are seen two soldiers of the 14th century, and in the back ground a view of Rochester Castle.

Many actions of this great man deserve the painter's attention; we mention the following as the most prominent.

The close of the battle of Crecy, when the Prince went to the King to receive the eulogium of his valour, and the triple plume of the King of Bohemia was laid at his father's feet. See Froissart.

His conversation with Sir James Audley and Sir John Chandos at Poitiers. Froissart.

His affecting meeting with Sir James Audley after the battle.   *Ibidem.*

His modest behaviour towards King John, his prisoner.   *Ibidem.*

The entrance of King John into London, attended by the Prince on a black hobby.

Ibidem.

The Battle of Navaretta.   *Ibidem.*

His sparing the inhabitants of Limoges on account of the valour of three French captains.   Thomas Walsingham.

AUTHORITIES.

The Prince and Arms from the tomb at Canterbury.
The Soldiers of the 14th century from 16. G. VI. Royal Library, B.M.

KING EDWARD III. IN HIS ROBES.

ANNO 1377.

The life and actions of this great Prince form a period no less interesting than glorious, in the annals of England. Inured from his youth to the turbulent factions of his nobles, he had the policy to convert their high and boisterous spirit, to the purposes of his own ambition. With a handsome person, and affable manners, he joined policy in counsel with the most heroic valour, and reigned for more than fifty years the terror and admiration of his neighbours. Although his conquests produced no solid aggrandisement of his dominions, the sea-fight off Sluys, and the battles of Duplin, Catsand, Halidown Hill, Crecy, Nevil's Cross, Poitiers, and Najara, cast so brilliant a beam of glory over his people, and kindled in their breasts so lasting a sense of superior prowess, as neither the lapse of ages, the pursuits of commerce nor the enervating effects of luxury, have ever been able to extinguish.

We have copied the annexed Costume and Portrait from the fine monumental effigy on the tomb of King Edward in Westminster Abbey, where the artist has expressed with remarkable felicity, the venerable beauty, sweetness, and dignity, recorded by historians, and coinciding with the ideas his great actions and character inspire.

The dress of the King consists of a long tunic, bordered with flowered lace, and lined with fur, open at the bottom as high as the knee. Between the opening below, and at the ends of the sleeves, appears an under garment, likewise laced. Over the shoulders is thrown a regal mantle enriched with fur and ornamented with lace. On the head of the statue, are the marks of a crown, now, as well as the sceptre, lost: both are restored from contemporary authorities, and the draperies coloured from similar subjects in the British Museum.

AUTHORITIES.

King Edward III. from the monument in Westminster Abbey. Crown from the monument of Henry III. and Sceptre from the picture of Richard II. in the Jerusalem Chamber. Throne and attendant from B.M.: Cotton, Nero, E. II.

C.H.S. del.

Etched by I.A.Atkinson

Aquatinted by R.&D.Havell

1377

Edward III King of
& Lord of Ireland

England and France
surnamed of Windsor

KING RICHARD II.

WITH AN ATTENDANT, SUPPOSED TO REPRESENT

JOAN PLANTAGENET, PRINCESS OF WALES AND COUNTESS OF KENT,

SURNAMED THE FAIR MAID OF KENT.

ANNO 1377.

This Princess was the daughter of Edmund of Woodstock, Earl of Kent, sixth and youngest son of King Edward I. She was born in 1328. After the death of her two brothers, in the 25th year of her age, she became Countess of Kent in her own right, being at the time married to Sir Thomas Holand, one of the Founders of the Garter. After his decease, she took for her second husband William Montague, Earl of Salisbury, but was divorced the same year by mutual consent,* 1361. Being now in her 33rd year, she still possessed so much beauty as to captivate, and soon after to marry, the Black Prince. By him, she had issue King Richard II. She outlived her third husband about nine years, and died in 1385 of affliction, because the king, her son, had refused to pardon his uterine brother, John Holand, who had been guilty of an atrocious murder. Notwithstanding that Walsingham has treated her character with little respect, and that the guilty ambition of the House of Lancaster has not scrupled to visit her memory with obloquy; her many amiable qualities gave her great influence with the people. Her popularity was so great, that by her intreaties alone she averted the vengeance of an exasperated mob, which had already plundered the Savoy palace, and threatened the life of John of Gaunt; and not only made his peace, but induced them quietly to disperse. This she did at a time, when she could not be ignorant of the intrigues of that very man to dethrone her son. At another time she was suffered to pass through the midst of a troop of rebels; and as long as she lived, the affection that was borne her, greatly contributed to support the government of her young and ill-advised son. But her exertions to maintain the internal peace of the kingdom greatly harassed her mind and fatigued her body, now grown extremely corpulent. In this state of health she received the shock of the stern though just resolution of the King, not to pardon his half-brother. She only survived the fatal news five days, although she might have reflected, that he did not possess sufficient firmness to persevere in such a vigorous determination; for soon after, without any ostensible cause, he granted that remission, which the intreaties of his dying parent and their common mother could not obtain.

It is rather remarkable, that the illumination from which the plate is copied, should have escaped the attention of Mr. Strutt, or that he should have failed to recognize in the portrait, the wife of the Black Prince, when he had

---

* According to Sandford; though it seems, that she was first married to the Earl of Salisbury, but having previously been contracted to Sir Thomas Holand, she was divorced and William (not Thomas Montacute, as Gough names him,) married another lady. Gough says she died in 1383.

already acknowledged another similar miniature in the same book for that of her husband.* Both represent King Richard, before the age of manhood, dressed in a tabbard of his arms, and attended by one of his parents with ducal coronets on their heads; but from the circumstance of the nimbi that surround them personifying saints. The Prince being habited in a robe *semé fleur de lys*, seems to represent St. Louis. The Princess, with a palm branch in her hand, and what appears to be a wheel at her feet, is probably in the character of St. Catherine. Why these two saints should have been selected as tutelary beings to the young king, it is not easy to determine. The figure, however, displays much sweetness, and though somewhat stout, certainly possesses beauty. Her hair is light, and dressed in two large tufts of ringlets on each side of her temples. Over her gown she wears a mantle. The nimbus, palm-branch, &c. not having any reference to the Costume have been omitted.

Arms. Parti per pale, France and England under a label of three points for Edward Prince of Wales, and *gules* three lions passant guardant *or* within a border *argent*, for E. of Woodstock, Earl of Kent, father to the Princess.

AUTHORITY.

From a Psalter, formerly the property of King Richard II., and probably presented to him by his mother, now in the Cottonian collection, B.M., marked Domitian, A. XVII.

* See Strutt's Dresses and Habits, Vol. II. Plate LXXXIV.

C.H.S. del.t   Etched by J.A. Atkinson.   Hill aquatinta.

Joane Plantaganet,  *Princefs of Wales,*
and Countefs of Kent *surnamed the fair Maid of Kent*

1377

COURTIERS ATTENDING ON THE KING.

ANNO 1377.

No sooner had the death of the Black Prince suspended the military enthusiasm of the English, than Richard, on ascending the throne, dismissed all the maxims and customs of his grandfather's court, a decided taste for dissipation excepted. Without the warlike qualities of his father, the political sagacity of one of his uncles, the austere firmness of another, or the hereditary ambition of a Plantagenet, he regarded his exalted situation only as the means of displaying his extravagance in processions and tournament, or of gratifying the unprincipled desires of his favourites. This love of gaudy shew, wandering without the guidance of taste, from the boundaries of civic virtue, and military propriety, soon begat extravagancies as ridiculous as they were contemptible. Rude splendour was mistaken for elegance. The most costly stuffs, cut and fashioned in every variety of shape, were squandered with tasteless profusion on the persons of all, whose births or fortunes were adequate to bear the expense.

But of all the fashions exhibited during this period of dissipation, none could vie, for inconvenience or awkwardness, with the long piked shoes then worn. It seems as if this absurd custom was a type of the frivolity and luxury of the princes during whose sway it was in vogue: the long-toed shoe began to be in fashion under William Rufus, was condemned by Henry I. encouraged by Richard II. tolerated under Henry VI. and finally proscribed by Edward IV. At the period now under consideration, fashion had lengthened the pike to the extent of eighteen inches beyond the end of the toe; and in order to enable the encumbered beau to lift his feet from the ground with tolerable security, chains of gold, silver, or of meaner metals, were fastened from their points to the knee, or even to the girdle. Thus King James I. of Scotland is represented with chains of gold fastening and peaks of his shoes to his girdle, in a full-length portrait at Kielberg, near Tubingen, in Swabia, the seat of the family of the Von Lytrums.

It is singluar that the extreme inconvenience of this fashion was insufficient to prevent its duration, or obstruct its revival. Yet the royal mandates, and the exhortations from the pulpit, long contended against this enormity without effect; nor was it until the fifth of Edward IV. that an act of parliament, enforced by a proclamation, finally reduced the shoe to the moderate length of two inches beyond the toe.

The plate represents two courtiers, selected from among the attendants on Richard II. about the period of his accession to the throne. They exhibit the piked shoes, kneechains, parti-coloured hose, golden collars, and circles round the head; the hair of both, in the original, is painted white, as if powder had already been in fashion at that period; but as no exact mention has been made of this practice by our early historians, the colouring is probably accidental.

AUTHORITY.

The figures are taken from an illumination in a MS. in the royal library at the British Museum, marked 20. B 6, written in the beginning of Richard II.

Officers of the Court of ROBERT DE VERE DUKE OF IRELAND *King Richard the Second.*

13 77

WILLIAM BEAUCHAMP, LORD BERGAVENNY.

ANNO 1392.

This figure is taken from an elegant painting on glass in the East window of St. Mary's Hall, Coventry. The fine outline of the head, its animation and character, denote it to be a portrait. He is represented in a state habit, with a hood of crimson embroidered with gold; his robe of a deep purple, lined with ermine and crimson, falls in ample folds round the body and feet. The girdle is richly studded; the sleeves and hose green; on the breast he wears a cross pattee of gold suspended by a golden chain; and over the left shoulder hangs a superb belt of gold and precious stones. I have nowhere met with the meaning of this ornament. Rouse, in his illuminations of the life and actions of Richard Earl of Warwick, has occasionally decorated his hero with it; the same ornament is also worn by several of the Earls of Holland, as painted in the church at Utrecht. This majestic and imposing costume seems to have been long in vogue; for specimens are found from the latter end of the reign of K. Richard II. to Edward IV.

Sir William Beauchamp was a partisan of John of Gaunt, and attended him in all his campaigns in France and Spain: he fought several actions at sea: was created Knight of the Garter, and appointed Captain of Calais. It was in this important command, when he suspected the views of Richard's favourites, that he refused, when ordered, to deliver up his government, and seized on the King's letters directed to the court of France. Afterwards, when John de la Pole, brother of Michael Earl of Suffolk, the great favourite, came to supersede him, in the government, he arrested and brought him a prisoner to England. The King was so incensed at this firm conduct, that he put him in confinement; but dreading some evil consequences, soon released him again.

He died in 1411, leaving his son Richard, afterwards Earl of Worcester, to succeed him. Vide Dugdale's Baronage, Froissart, &c.

This distinguished character may be introduced in many of the historic scenes of the reigns of Edward III. Richard II. and Henry IV.

Back-ground. A view of Calais from the sea, as it was in the middle of the 16th century.

AUTHORITIES.

The figure from the painted glass, supposed to have been executed by John Thornton, painter and glass-stainer of Coventry, a man of great merit; the same who executed the great eastern window of York Minster, between the years 1405 and 1407.

The views of Calais from Hollar's print, compared with a rare German print without marks, of the siege of that place tempore Elizabeth.

Sir William Beauchamp   K.^TG.^R *Lord Bergavenny*
Captain of Calais, Custos   *of the County of Pembroke*

13 92

ARTHUR MACMURROCH, OR MAQUEMORE,

KING OF LEINSTER.—ANNO 1399.

Froissart, while relating the wars of King Richard II. in Ireland, mentions the subject of this Plate in a very curious narrative, which, when coupled with that of Francis de la Marque, who was an eyewitness to the second campaign, throws sufficient light upon this singular character to enable us to give some idea of his talents for war and negotiation. It appears that Macmurroch, or Maquemore, as the French Chronicles have styled him, was one of the most powerful, if not the head of the confederate chieftains, who opposed the great expedition led by King Richard in the year 1395. Sensible of the insufficiency of open resistance against so powerful an adversary, and that safety was only to be obtained by creating delays till the hostile army should withdraw, he, with his companions, feigning to listen to the proposals of the Earl of Ormond, suffered himself to be allured to Dublin, where he patiently underwent the discipline of learning to eat in the English fashion, to wear breeches and fur gowns, and at length of receiving knighthood from the hand of Richard himself. As foreseen, the English forces departed with their king at the end of the summer to enjoy the honours of imaginary conquest, while Macmurroch returned to his native fastnesses with substantial independence. Richard at length convinced of the inutility of his first measures, went over a second time, at the head of a powerful army, in the year 1399, and opposed to the wary Hibernian the conduct and valour of Thomas Despencer Earl of Gloucester. During the former expedition, the actions of the chieftain had been confounded with those of his colleagues, but on this occasion he stood alone. Aware that his faithless behaviour would not safely admit of a repetition, he now posted himself securely in the mountains at the head of an army, and from this commanding station had the address to entice even the gallent Earl into conferences on equal terms. Here he spun out the time till the unfortunate Monarch's adversities increased, and he at length discovered, that so far from conquering a kingdom, his crown and sceptre had already passed into the hands of an usurper.

AUTHORITY.

The manuscript of Francis de la Marque, in the Harleian Library, British Museum, marked 1319.

Arthur Mc Murroch   *King of Leinster.*

THE
KING BETRAYED BY THE EARL OF NORTHUMBERLAND.

ANNO 1399.

King Richard having been induced to quit Conway Castle, by the base and artful persuasions of Henry Percy, first Earl of Northumberland, consented to go and meet the Duke of Lancaster; hoping, though conscious of the injuries he had done him, that his crown and life would still be secure. Under the guidance of the Earl he quitted the castle, and having crossed the water, proceeded towards Rutland. Percy, who, under the pretence of preparing dinner, had gone before, laid an ambush in a pass between a steep rock and the sea: here he awaited the King's approach, and having secured his person conducted him to Chester. Francis de la Marque, before quoted, relates the subject somewhat different from Stowe, and it seems that, though an eyewitness, he has confounded the names of Rutland and Chester together.

The King is dressed in a scarlet robe, a black hood, and having his beard long, probably with an intent to disguise himself. The Earl and his soldiers are in armour with flowered loose surcoats, which seems to indicate that the use of emblazoned coats, as worn in the reign of Edward the Third, had been laid aside. He is bare-headed, and holds a battle-axe in his hand.

AUTHORITY.

Francis de la Marque in the B.M.: Harleian 1319.

Percy
1399

King Richard
betrayed by the Earl

the Second
of Northumberland.

ROGER WALDEN, BISHOP OF LONDON.

ANNO 1405.

This prelate first appears to have been dean of York. He was admitted Prebendary of Gillingham, in the diocese of Salisbury, in January 1392; September, same year, collated to a prebend in the diocese of Exeter, being then treasurer of Calais. Afterwards secretary to Richard II., and subsequently treasurer of England, which high office he resigned September 20, 1395.–On February 10th, 1397, he was admitted to the prebend of Wilesdon, in St. Paul's cathedral. In 1398, in consequence of Archbishop Arundel having been banished the kingdom, Walden was promoted to the vacant see of Canterbury; but upon the deposition of Richard II., the Pope (who favoured Arundel) pronounced him an intruder and usurper of the archbishopric, and by his bull restored Arundel. Walden was thus a bishop without a bishopric, and so continued about two years, when by the kind endeavours of Archbishop Arundel, he was appointed to the vacant see of London; which, however, he enjoyed for a very short period: that mitre was bestowed upon him December 10, 1404;* he was installed June 30, 1405, and he died June 6th following: he was interred in the priory of St. Bartholomew in Smithfield.

The figure is copied from a painting on glass in St. Mary's Hall, Coventry; where Walden is placed by the side of his benefactor Arundel: from their having a place in this hall, it is evident that both were members, and perhaps benefactors, of the Trinity Gild, which probably happened in October, 6th of Henry IV.; for the king assembled a parliament in that year at Coventry, (which acquired the name of *Parliamentum indoctorum*, or the laymen's parliament.) Archbishop Arundel was present, and much distinguished himself by his spirited conduct and energetic speech in defence of the church. It is presumed that Walden attended; for though the date of his elevation to the see of London is stated by Godwin to be December 10, yet in fact the Papal bull only is of that date; and as Braybroke died 28th August, 1404, it is not unlikely that Walden was nominated previous to the parliament held at Coventry, and attended as Bishop of London. The short period he enjoyed that dignity, allows of no other public occasion for his visiting Coventry; and as the two prelates are placed together in the same window, the conjecture almost amounts to proof.

AUTHORITIES.

From a painting on glass in the windows of St. Mary's Hall, Coventry. For the whole of this article I am indebted to Mr. Thomas Sharp of Coventry: the back-ground is ideal, though the materials are taken from existing architectural remains.

* The Pope's "bulla provisionis" bears this date.

C.H.S. dd.t   Etched by I.A.Atkinson.   Aquatinted by Hill.

Roger Walden.   *Bishop of London.*

1405.

JOHN CROSBIE, PRIOR OF COVENTRY.

ANNO 1407—8.

This is the only representation of a mitred prior, *in pontificalibus*, that has come under my observation in this kingdom, and considering the circumstance that he was living on the spot when the figure was painted, it is highly probable that the artist has endeavoured to exhibit his portrait. The probability is increased when the features of the face are considered; and it is observed, that his apparent youth coincides with the time when the supposed artist flourished, which was some years before the actual death of his subject. He is habited in a loose gown of a deep blue colour, exactly resembling that which is worn by Archbishop Thomas à Becket, in the ancient picture preserved in Canterbury Cathedral; of which Mr. Carter has given a correct representation. The crosier (as is usual in the monumental representations of mitred abbots,) he holds in his left hand, and with his right he sustains a book, which may be emblematic of his studies, or of some literary production of his pen. The prior's mitre is no ways inferior in splendor to that of a bishop, and the whole figure conveys an idea of magnificence not unsuitable to a dignitary who had a seat in the parliament of England.

Of the personal history of Crosbie nothing is known. In the series of priors, he is only remarkable for having governed nearly forty years, succeeding Roger Cotton in 1399, and dying in 1436.

AUTHORITIES.

Both the figure and arms from the painting on glass in St. Mary's Hall, Coventry. For this account of Crosbie, I am obliged to Mr. T. Sharp of that city.

John Crosbie *Prior of Coventry.*

1407.8.

SIR WILLIAM GASCOIGNE,

CHIEF JUSTICE OF THE KING'S BENCH IN THE REIGN OF KING HENRY V.

ANNO 1413.

We cannot present a better biographical sketch of this justly celebrated character, than by transcribing the account which Mr. Gough has extracted from the Biographia Britannica, and published with the description of his monument.*

"Sir William Gascoigne was descended from an ancient family, in which he had seven predecessors of his surname, and is supposed to have been born about 1350. He was made a King's Sergeant in the end of Richard the Second's reign, 1398; and appointed by that king one of the Attorneys for Henry, Duke of Lancaster, in his exile; which grant was revoked by the same king; and regranted by Hentry IV. on his accession to the crown. Throughout his reign, Gascoigne's arguments and decisions occur in our year books, and he was appointed Chief Justice of the King's Bench Nov. 15, 1401; having before sat in the Common Pleas. He was in the commission for levying forces aginst the Earl of Northumberland's insurrection, 1403; and for treating with his associates, and receiving them to mercy on payment of their fines, 1405; and again, 1408, he incurred the King's displeasure by declining sitting in judgment on Archbishop Scrope; but soon after recovered it, and received the honour of knighthood."

He was twice married, first to Elizabeth, heiress of Alexander Mowbray; and, secondly, to Joan, daughter of Sir William Pickering.

The figure is copied from a sketch made some years ago by a friend, from an altar tomb in Harwood Church, Yorkshire. The original lies in a recumbent attitude with hands conjoined. His head is covered with a hood or capucium fitting so close that the ears under it are distinguishable; the cope, which seems to have been in general use in the reigns of Henry IV. and V.† is seen below the mantle, on the breast, reaching to the arm-pits. Over his robes he wears a mantle, buttoned on the right shoulder. The loose sleeves and skirt of his robe are lined with ermine: below are strait sleeves buttoned close to the wrist. His belt has a large buckle, from whence hangs a narrow end studded with roses. On his right side he wears an aunelace, and on his left a purse, ornamented with tassels. The wand in his right hand is ideal.

AUTHORITIES.

The monument in Harwood Church, Yorkshire. The gilt railing behind formerly in the great hall of the old court at Brussels. The colouring of the robes after an illumination of a judge on the bench in a MS. of the 14th century in the British Museum, marked Royal, 15. D. III.

* Gough's Sepulchral Monuments, Vol. II. page 37.
† Both these kings have this garment on their monuments at Canterbury and Westminster.

C.H.S. del.ᵗ   Etched by I.A.Atkinson.   Aquatinted by Havel.

Sir William Gascoigne  *Kᵗ. Chief Justice of the*
King's *Bench.*

1413

ROBERT CHAUMBERLEYN, ESQUIRE TO THE KING.

ANNO 1417.

Wᵉ have searched in vain for particulars, concerning the life and character of the person, whose portrait and costume is represented in the annexed plate. It is said that he was present at the battle of Azincourt; a circumstance very probable, as an entry in the book of benefactors to the Abbey of St. Alban's* proves, not only that he was an Esquire to the King, but also a boon companion with the monks.

The design is extremely interesting on account of its offering one of the most complete specimens of a man at arms fully equipped for battle, belonging to this period of history, in existence. In order to place the figure in a more characteristic view, the kneeling posture of the original has been altered to a standing attitude; and the shield, which in the illumination is represented on the margin, has, agreeably to other contemporary drawings, been hung on the neck. The battle-axe is added from a miniature in a copy of Froissart's Chronicles at the British Museum.

The warrior appears in a helmet with a moveable vizor over his skull-cap and gorget of mail; his surcoat is cloth of silver flowered of the same, without any armorial bearings and as a simple esquire, unauthorized to wear gold, his spurs, belt, and the pummels of his sword and dagger are of plain silver.

AUTHORITIES.

The figure see note.* Battle-axe: Royal 18, E 2. Arms, Ashmole's History of the Order of the Garter.

* The entry is by the side of the illumination from which the costume is copied, and may be translated in the following words: "In the year of grace 1417, on the day after the crucifixion, Robert surnamed Chaumberleyn, Esquire of our Lord the King, was received into the fraternity of our chapter, and on that day he gave a liberal donation of wine to the convent." Accordingly the gratitude of the jolly monks caused his portrait to be painted in the book of benefactors. Bibliotheca Cottoniana, Nero, D. VII.

Robert Chaumberloyn

Esquire to the King

Ch. Sdt.

Etch'd by I.A.Atkinson

Aquatinted by J.Hill

Sir Thomas Erpingham

A LADY OF THE REIGN OF KING HENRY V.

ANNO 1420.

The subject of the Plate before us represents a costume, which, by displaying the neck and shoulders to advantage, and exhibiting the symmetry of the body and sweep of the limbs, must have been fraught with no common attractions. The head dress is of the crescent or horned kind, though not the frightful fashion which obtained in the reign of Edward IV. This before us is first observable in MSS. of the latter end of the fourteenth century. It occurs again in a painting on glass, in St. Mary's Hall, Coventry; which, if the received opinion of the time when it was painted be correct, must be referred to the beginning of the fifteenth century. Like all other female fashions, this mode of decorating the head underwent constant and rapid alterations. Isabella of Bavaria introduced in France the high sugar-loaf caps sometimes rising into single spires, at others dividing into two lobes like a heart, and generally embellished with long veils.

In the original illumination, from whence the design is copied, the lady holds in her hands the shields of arms of Burgundy. She is placed in a vignette page of a book, surrounded by angels playing on various instruments: among others is one with a dulcimer, which, being an object of some curiosity and not unbecoming the attitude or the character of the female figure, I have transferred into her hands instead of the escutcheon. From the style and form of the letters, the book was evidently written in the beginning of the fifteenth century; and the arms of Burgundy being placed under the principal illuminations, point out that family as the original owners; and, perhaps, Anne, daughter of John Duke of Burgundy, who married to the great Duke of Bedford in 1423, was the person through whose possession it passed into the hands of the English. The castle and back-ground are ideal.

AUTHORITY.

From a beautiful missal in the Harleian Library, British Museum, marked 2897.

C.H.S. del.

Etch'd by I.L. Atkinson

Aquatinted by Hill

John Duke of Bedford
1420

A Lady of the reign *of King Henry V*

RALPH NEVILLE, FIRST EARL OF WESTMORLAND,

LORD OF RABY CASTLE, BRANSPETH, WARKWORTH, &C. K.G.

AND HIS SECOND WIFE, JOAN BEAUFORT, DAUGHTER OF

JOHN OF GAUNT, DUKE OF LANCASTER.

ANNO 1425—6.

Ralph Neville, descended from Gospatrick, Earl of Northumberland, was the first of that name, who attained the rank of an Earl. In the ninth of Richard II. he was Governor of the West Marches, towards Scotland, and soon after Warden of the King's Forests beyond Trent for life. Twenty-first of Richard, being one of the privy council, he was created Earl of Westmorland and Constable of the Tower of London. But he deserted Richard, and joined Henry Duke of Lancaster, at Ravenspur, and was by him constituted Earl Marshal, with the gift of the county of Richmond for life.

The Earl of Westmorland is introduced in Shakespeare's historical plays of Henry IV. He was twice married: first to Margaret, daughter of Hugh, Earl of Strafford, by whom he had issue two sons and seven daughters. His second wife was Joan, daughter of John of Gaunt, Duke of Lancaster, and he had issue by her eight sons and five daughters.

The figure of the Earl exhibits a fine specimen of the armour, as it was worn by the great, from the middle of the reign of Edward III. to the end of Henry IV.* His vambraces, gauntlets, cuisses, knee-pieces and greaves are edged with rich seams of fretwork. A superb military girdle, studded with pearls, &c. encircles his hips, and over that is a belt from which his sword is suspended. His skull-cap, of a pointed form, is elegantly wrought round the borders, with the Gothic letters I.H.S. embossed on the front. Round the cap is a wreath or torse, embroidered with leaves. He wears a huge pair of whiskers, his gorget is of mail, and round the neck he has a collar of SS. In his right hand he holds a battle-axe of state, and behind him, on a cushion, is the tilting helmet, surmounted with his crest. On his left hand is Joan Beaufort, his second wife, habited in a splendid mantle and coronet and collar of SS. The back-ground is ideal, and the battle-axe has been added for the sake of attitude.

AUTHORITIES.

Both the figures and the helmet from a drawing taken from the monumental effigies in alabaster, and formerly painted and gilt, in Staindrop Church, in the county of Durham. The battle-axe from a painting on glass formerly in a window of St. Mary's Hall, Coventry. (See the figure of the Earl of Stafford, etched by Hollar, in Dugdale's Warwickshire.)

* The effigy itself affords a proof, that this kind of armour was worn after that period; there are some later even to the end of the wars of the Roses, but in the last instances, I am inclined to think, that this elegant costume had, in some measure, become monumental.

Ralph Nevill 1st Earl of   *Westmorland, Lord of Raby Castle,*

Earl Marshall,   *Kt of the Garter, &c. &c.*

and his second Wife   *Joan Beaufort.*

14   26.

JOAN PICKERING, LADY GASCOIGNE.

ANNO 1429.

We consider this Figure as the representation of Joan, the second wife of Sir William Gascoigne, and think, with Mr. Lethieuillier, that the date, 1429, mentioned by Mr. Oldys, refers to her. The head-dress of females of fashion was, in the latter part of the reign of Edward the Third, reticulated upon two perpendicular cylinders, pendent on each side of the head; these cylinders became shorter and wider, in the reign of Richard, and were, at last, loosened and thrown in tufts of curls, like the head of Joan, the fair maid in Kent, before published. In the reign of Henry IV. they were again gathered in net-work, of an orbicular shape, as may be seen in the effigy of Joan of Navarre, queen of that sovereign, the two wives of the Earl of Westmorland, and many others. They, afterwards, were flattened out horizontally, as in the specimen before us, until, at length, in the reign of Henry VI the extremities were turned up, and finally produced the horned head-dress. Over the net-work is cast a veil, with a fringed border, hanging down behind upon the shoulders. On the top of her head is a kind of wreath, embroidered with flowers, and in the middle, above the forehead, something like a jewel, upon which is represented a crane in the act of pecking, which possibly may be allusive to the name of Pickering. Mr. Gough says, "she has a mantle, with a deep falling cape buttoned over the breast, with a broad belt and large buckle round the waist, which is short, the gown under it is plaited before, &c." He should have said, that she is habited in an ample gown, with a falling cape, probably of fur, laced down the breast, and having long and wide sleeves, resembling the female costumes in Strutt's Dresses and Habits, Plate CXIX. And that of Joan Perient, as represented on her brass plate, at Digswell, C. Hertford, under the date of 1415. The colouring of the costume is taken from one of the contemporary figures in Strutt's Plate CXIX.

AUTHORITY.

From the monument in Harwood Church, Yorkshire.

CHS. del.   Etch'd by I.A.Atkinson.   Aquatinted by Hill.

Joan Pickering   *Lady Gascoyne.*

Pickering

1413.

CECILIA, LADY BRYAN STAPLETON.

ANNO 1432.

Although the brass plate from which this Costume is taken appears formal and stiff, there is much real elegance in the draperies when represented in living attitude and motion. The head dress is reticulated, and covered with a veil. The gown close, with long and narrow sleeves; the mantle being seldom represented in the illuminations of this period, ought to be considered, on this and other monumental figures, as a mere state costume. Cecilia, wife of Sir Bryan Stapleton, was daughter of William, Lord Bardolf, and died September 29, 1432.

AUTHORITY.

From a brass plate in Ingham Church, Norfolk.

Etched by I.A.Atkinson.

Cecilia Lady of Sir   *Bryan Stapleton K.G.*

A SPORTSMAN OF RANK, AND GAME-KEEPER.

ANNO 1435.

The figure before us, representing a Sportsman of distinction, is copied from a beautiful small folio, conjectured to have been illuminated by the same hand which embellished the celebrated Bedford missal; as the costumes and drawings of the draperies, the colours, and the general execution of the ornaments, bear strong marks of resemblance. The subject of the original design is St. Eustace, or St. Hubert, kneeling upon his hat before a stag, having a cross between his antlers. The attitude of genuflexion occurs so often, and is so destitute of the advantages required to display costume, that we have not hesitated to convert it into a standing posture. The dress of the Sportsman consists of a scarlet jacket, with puffed and full sleeves, in conformity to a fashion introduced about the close of the reign of King Henry IV. and which, although in vogue for near half a century, was far from being elegant; the extreme width of shoulders, and seeming corpulence of body, seldom corresponding with the slender appearance of the legs. His hose are tight and of a black colour, with pointed toes, and his spurs have necks of immoderate length. His hat is in appearance not unlike those of modern times, and probably of felt. It must be observed of this part of the dress, that the crowns were at this period sufficiently strong to bear the weight of the body, as there are numerous instances of figures kneeling upon them without their yielding. He wears a horn suspended by a belt over the shoulder, and a long narrow sword by another round the hips.

Before the Sportsman stands a Game-keeper dressed in a white frock and boots, with a broad bawdrik slung over his shoulder, to which is suspended a hunter's horn. There is some singularity in his two girdles, the one round the waist, the other lower down, seemingly to gird up the skirts of his frock. In his left hand he holds a short boar spear, in his right the hind leg of a deer.

AUTHORITIES.

The Sportsman and horse from an elegant missal in the possession of Messrs. Gordon and Forster of St. Martin's Lane. The Game-keeper from the British Museum, marked Cotton: Augustus, A. 5, le tresor des histoires. The deer and back-ground are ideal.

C.H.S. del.

Aquatinted by Havell.

A Sportsman of Quality   *and Gamekeeper of the*
reign of   *King Henry 6.ᵗʰ*

Nevill 1.ard
Falconbridge.

RICHARD BEAUCHAMP, EARL OF WARWICK,

LIEUTENANT-GENERAL OF THE REALM OF FRANCE, GOVERNOR OF
NORMANDY AND CAPTAIN OF CALAIS, K.B. AND K.G.

ANNO 1439.

The subject of the Costume before us, was one of the most illustrious among a family distinguished for a series of heroes, whose fame contributed more to extend the military reputation of their country than that of any other, the Plantagenets excepted. Richard Beauchamp, Earl of Warwick, son of Earl Thomas, was born in 1381. At the coronation of Henry IV. he was made a Knight of the Bath, and about four years after a Knight of the Garter. He became Governor to the infant King Henry VI., and on the death of the great Duke of Bedford, he was appointed Lieutenant-General of the realm of France and the Dutchy of Normandy. He defeated the Duke of Burgundy, and raised the siege of Calais. He founded the chantry-chapel at Guy's-cliff, and a college at Elmley. The magnificent chapel at Warwick was built by his orders for the burial of himself and family. In the patent constituting him instructor to Henry VI., his fidelity, prudence, probity, good morals, and diligence are particularly noticed. He died in 1439, having by his first wife, Elizabeth, daughter and heiress of Thomas Lord Berkeley, three daughters; and by his second wife, Isabel, daughter of J. Le Despencer, Earl of Gloucester, Henry his son, afterwards Duke of Warwick, and a daughter, who at length became heiress of this powerful family, and carried the Earldom of Warwick into the House of Nevill, by her marriage with the celebrated Richard Nevill the king-maker.

The Earl is cased in a full suit of plate-armour, with high pass-guards and the joints of the left elbow-piece curiously shaped, so as to form a kind of shield, when the arm was bent in the natural position for holding the bridle. His hair is curled and cropped. He wears both sword and dagger suspended from the armour without any belt. On his left leg is the Garter. Below is the tilting helmet surmounted with a swan's head and neck, the crest of Beauchamp. In the back-ground is a war-horse caparisoned in emblazoned trappings of Beauchamp quartering Newburgh, the ancient Earls of Warwick. The groom and attendants bear the ragged staff on the breast and shoulders; which was the badge, or more properly part of the badge, of the ancient Earls. One holds the banner and another the pennon.

AUTHORITY.

The Earl and helmet from the elegant monumental figure in the Warwick chapel adjoining the collegiate church, at Warwick. The horse, attendants, and banners from the MS. life by John Rouse in the B.M. marked Cotton, Julius, E. IV. The arms from the monument above quoted.

C.H.S. del.ᵗ   Etched by I.A.Atkinson.   Aquatinted by Hill.

Richard Beauchamp,      *K.G. Earl of Warwick*

Regent of France   *Governor of Normandy*

and Captain   *of Calais.*

14 39

JOYCE LADY TIPTOFT AND POWIS.

ANNO 1446.

Jocosa, or Joyce, Lady Tiptoft, was daughter and co-heiress of Edward Charlton, Lord Powis, and Eleanor, daughter of Thomas Holland, Earl of Kent. She was born in 1404. Her husband, Sir John Tiptoft, nephew to Robert, the last Lord of the elder branch of his family, was a man of great consequence, and employed in various important stations. He bore the titles of Lord Tiptoft and Powis, and in right of his wife had summons to parliament 20th of Henry VI. They had issue, one only son John, the learned and unfortunate Earl of Worcester. Lady Joyce died in the forty-second year of her age, anno 1446.

Her costume consists of a reticulated head-dress and coronet, richly studded with jewels, with a short veil hanging on the neck behind. Her necklace is splendid, and adorned with a jewel pendent from the middle. She wears a surcoat and kirtle faced with ermine; and over the shoulders a mantle of her paternal arms, Powis impaling Holland, fastened by a rich cordon with tassels, and lined with fur; the whole having a superb appearance. This dress is frequently found depicted in illuminations of this period with the exception of the coronet and mantle, which ought to be regarded as part of a state apparel, in the same manner as the coronets and emblazoned surcoats on the armed monumental effigies of men of distinction of that and earlier times.

AUTHORITIES.

From the monumental brass plate in Enfield church Middlesex. The Arms from the same. For a detailed account of this lady, her monument, &c. see Gough's Sepulchral Monuments, Vol. II. p. 136.

C.H.S delt.

Etch'd by I.A. Atkinson

Tiptoft

Powys

1446

Ivoasa or Ioice Lady Tiptoft and Powys.

MILITARY COSTUMES

OF THE REIGN OF KING HENRY VI.

ANNO 1447.

The groups of warriors in the annexed Plate are copied from drawings in the original MS. life of St. Edmund, translated by Dan John Lydgate, monk of Bury, in order to be presented by him to King Henry VI., on his visit to that abbey, which we believe was in the year 1447.* They represent the grotesque, and almost absurd military costumes prevalent in that period, when the more simple and more martial habits of the heroic age of England were laid aside, and the Italian and Lombard fashions became prevalent. We must, however, own that in the original the figures with turbans are mostly intended to represent the enemies of St. Edmund, or, in other words, Pagans, and that, by a very natural association of ideas, the illuminator has possibly represented Turks, the Pagans of his time. It does not seem, that either Mr. Strutt or the author of the Harleian Catalogue have adverted to this circumstance, nor does our remark imply more than mere conjecture. Two of the soldiers in the foreground are armed with battle-axes, a third holds a gisarme, and the fourth a spear. Further back is one with an instrument like a halbert, and a large scimitar. The tents are richly ornamented, the disposition of the groups and back-ground are ideal.

AUTHORITY.

From the MS. above mentioned now in the Harleian Collection, marked 2278.

---

* The MS. was presented to King Henry, when he spent his Christmas at Bury. There is an illumination in the book, which represents the person of the King as not more than sixteen years of age; but as I have not found any other visit in which he spent his Christmas there, than that in 1447, when he likewise held a parliament there, I have fixed the dates of the Costumes to that year. Vide Stowe, black-letter edition, page 386.

C.H.S. del.

Etched by I.A. Atkinson.

Aquatinted by Hill.

Military costumes of the reign of King Henry VI
1447.

KING HENRY VI. AT HIS DEVOTIONS.

ANNO 1450.

The splendid, though neglected tapestry, of St. Mary's Hall at Coventry, from which the annexed subject of costume is taken, offers a variety of materials, no less interesting on account of the sanctity and misfortunes of the Prince, who is there represented, than curious as specimens of the arts of drawing, dying, and embroidery of the time in which it was executed.

"The right hand lower compartment, from which the annexed design is copied, shews the king kneeling at a covered table, on which is placed his arched crown and a missal. Behind him Cardinal Beauford in the same attitude, and a number of personages of rank and consequence standing. The opposite division exhibits Queen Margaret with a crown on her head and richly habited. There is great spirit in the countenance, though injured by having been mended at the corner of the mouth. Perhaps this is the only authentic portrait of this celebrated queen. Among the various female attendants which constitute the remainder of the groupe, some are splendidly dressed and adorned with chains of gold, while others are in the proper habits of nuns."*

The King wears on his head a cap of crimson velvet adorned with a button or jewel. The gown is of a sky blue colour richly embroidered with gold; round the neck hangs a golden chain of clumsy workmanship and enormous size. The arched crown asserted to have been first worn by him rests on the table. Behind the King are placed two figures selected from among those on the tapestry. One with a long beard, a jewel in the hat, and a golden collar of something like SS round the neck, and next to him a person in a long green gown holding a gold coin in his hand, no doubt intended to represent the King's almoner.

The back ground shews the inside of the north-west end of St. Michael's church at Coventry.

Arms. The royal arms of King Henry VI. with the arched crown on the top, supported by the silver antelopes, and at bottom the red roses of the house of Lancaster.

AUTHORITY.

The St. Mary Hall tapestry at Coventry.

* The annals of Coventry record, that in 1450 the King "with many lords," after following the Bishop of Winchester, "arrayed in his pontificals, and attended by the priests and clerks of the city in their copes," on Michaelmas day, in solemn procession round St. Michael's church-yard, went "into his closette" purposely prepared in the church, where he heard mass. Afterwards "at evening time" the King sent the gown which he wore in the said proccession, being of gold tissue furred with martin sable, as a free gift to God and St. Michael, in so much that the yeomen of his body, who brought the gown, would receive no reward. At this visit the King also granted great privileges to the city, making the bailiffs sheriffs, &c. and forming Coventry into a distinct county.

C.H.S. delt.   Etched by I.A.Atkinson   Aquatinted by R. Havell

Henry 6.th King of *England & France*
and Lord of Ireland *surnamed of Windsor.*

1450

QUEEN MARGARET OF ANJOU.

ANNO 1450.

In the preceding Number, under the head of Costume of King Henry VI. an account has been given of the tapestry, from which both that and the present subjects are selected.

Queen Margaret, the daughter of René, Duke of Anjou and titular King of Sicily, with considerable beauty, and some talents, was a prey to all the anxieties, the vicissitudes, and the disappointments of political intrigue. Her history, replete with incidents of opposite natures, impresses the mind with contradictory ideas of her character. Ambitious, crafty, spirited, inconstant, cruel and implacable, she excites horror; beautiful, eloquent, and injured; intrepid in the cause of her husband; tender in that of her son, she appears a heroine. But compared with other female characters, who have borne conspicuous parts in English history, she was neither affectionate, like Eleanor; respectable, like Philippa; lovely, like the Queen of Scots; nor majestic, like Elizabeth; she strove singly to bear the weight of her husband's crown, and sunk under the burthen.

The annexed plate represents her with an animated countenance; the crowned head-dress and veil studded with pearls, is both rich and elegant. Her gown is cloth of gold. Her attitude on the tapestry is somewhat low, as if kneeling on a bench, with both hands joined in prayer: for the sake of variety, her figure is here represented standing, with the left hand elevated, so as to enable the observer to remark the slender waists then in fashion. Behind the Queen are several ladies of the Court, with varied head-dresses. The back ground is ideal. The shield on the pillar, the armorial bearing of Edward Charleton Lord Powis, 102d Knight of the Garter.

Little is to be gathered for the painter in the annals of court intrigue. The mysteries of these transactions are either unfit or unworthy of the pencil; hence few incidents in the life of this Princess afford scope for composition. We may except the scene with the robber in the wood, after the battle of Hexham. *Vide Hall's Chronicle.*

Queen Margaret's reconciliation with the King-making Earl of Warwick. *Shakespeare.*

Her conduct when captured after the battle of Tewkesbury. *Hall's Chronicle. Hutton's Bosworth Field.*

AUTHORITIES

The tapestry in St. Mary's Hall, Coventry.
Arms. Vide Sandford.

Margaret of Anjou, Queen   *to King Henry the 6th*

14 50

JOHN LORD BEAUMONT,

CONSTABLE, AND LORD HIGH CHAMBERLEYN OF ENGLAND.

ANNO 1450.

With the representations of King Henry VI. and Queen Margaret of Anjou, we have entered into some details respecting the tapestry, from which they, as well as the subject under consideration, are copied. The courtier, whose figure is here exhibited, has been presumed to represent Lord Beaumont, on account of the prominence of his station in the King's compartment; a preference likely to be bestowed on a personage not only most conspicuous for favour with that prince and his queen, but also an object of particular affection to the city; the arms of which he bore on his crest. He was held in this loyal place, the most trusty adviser of his master, and at the time under consideration, his influence and power were so great, that in the very hall, where this curious original is still visible, in a parliament there assembled, he caused those hostile acts to pass against the House of York, which, in the end, produced the terrible wars of the two roses. In all likelyhood, his interest procured particular favours for the city,* commemorated by the grateful inhabitants in the tapestry so often alluded to. To these general probabilities might be added the age and splendid appearance of the courtier, and the embroidered sachel suspended to his girdle. This latter accompaniment is seldom represented so highly ornamented, unless upon the persons of the chancellor, treasurer, or steward of a sovereign. As the chancellors during the reign of Henry VI. were all, with the exception of one, ecclesiastics, the sachel must here refer to either of the other offices, and both might be said to have been in the posession of this nobleman, of whom we will give a short account.†

The costume consists of a coat of cloth of gold fringed with silver, and a gown of a light blue colour bordered with pink. On the head is worn a cap similar to that of the King, but without button or jewel. Behind are two more courtiers in different habits. In the back-ground a view of St. Mary's Hall at Coventry.

AUTHORITIES

The tapestry before quoted. The back-ground taken on the spot.

---

* "The King also granted great privileges to the city, making the bailiffs sheriffs, and giving them jurisdiction independent of the county of Warwick, forming Coventry, with certain adjoining hamlets and parishes, into a distinct county." *Vide the note at the end of King Henry VI.*

† One of the most conclusive arguments for fixing the date of the execution of the tapestry is founded on the necessity of its having been finished before the destruction of the Lancastrian party, as neither Edward IV. nor Richard III. would have permitted such tribute of attachment to be produced during their reigns, and had it been after the accession of Henry VII. when it was the fashion to call Henry VI. a saint, his partisans would undoubtedly have placed a nimbus round his head, a distinction often conferred in those days, on worthies of more questionable character. It must therefore have been made between 1450 and 1460.

Courtier of the reign   *of King Henry VI.*

supposed to represent John Viscount   *Beaumont K.G. Earl of Boulogne*

Constable & Lord High   *Chamberlain of England.*

1450.

Etched by J.A. Atkinson.

Aquatinted by Havell.

A TOURNAMENT.

AS PRACTISED IN THE FIFTEENTH CENTURY.

ANNO 1450.

Justs and tournaments began to be practised in the 12th century. They were the organised offspring of the Trojan Game, Battaillole, Emprise, Pardons d'Armes, and Behourdis, all terms originally employed to designate simulated combats, practised for the purpose of military instruction. It seems that the politic and valiant Theodoric first brought these sports into notice at Rome, by substituting them to the shews of the gladiators. In the beginning they were mere exercises to accustom the martial youth of Europe to the management of their horses and the dextrous handling of their weapons, but in process of time they became regular exhibitions; and after the ladies were permitted to view them and to bestow the rewards of valour, they soon were converted into the most splendid, as well as the most warlike, amusement of the chivalrous ages.

Anno 920. The Emperor Henry, the Fowler, gave one of these military feasts; when the combatants fought on horseback. Towards the conclusion of the 11th century, Geoffry de Preuilly, a knight of Touraine, first introduced some regulations for their celebration. In the reign of King Stephen* they were known in England, but tournaments, only, became common in the time of Richard I. From that period, to the end of Elizabeth, they continued the delight and boast of our nobility: but Henry II., of France, having been killed in a just, in 1559; and Prince Henry, of Bourbon Montpensier, meeting with a similar fate, the year after, they were reluctantly laid aside, occasionally revived in the Pas d'Armes, or faintly retraced in the simple amusement of running at the ring.

The Plate represents a tournament, or, more properly, a just, as practised in the middle of the 15th century. In the centre is seen one of the challengers or tenants of the lists, bearing his tilting spear into the shield of his opponent, who is represented on the opposite side of the barrier, with his lance shivered to pieces. Both are attended by their respective esquires, whose business it was to reach them fresh lances, and to assist them in re-mounting, when they had the misfortune to be thrown. In the back-ground, to the left, are the crimson pavilions of the tenants, with their peace and war shields suspended upon them, for the opponents to touch, when they claimed the combat according to the laws of arms. Between the tents are two more tenants of the field, ready armed, and waiting with their esquires and pages behind them, for a summons from the opposite side. A cord is stretched before the horses, to prevent their entering the lists before their turn. In the corner of the field, at the eastern gate, are three heralds, holding the banners of the three tenants and decorated with the blason of their arms. On the right side of the Plate sites the sovereign, or principal person, in whose presence the tournament is held, accompanied by ladies. He holds a white wand, which, when he dropped, the combat was to cease. Below him are seen, on one side, the trumpeters of the solemnity; on the other, the judges and heralds to record and

---

* According to Robert of Gloucester, William Rufus was an able tilter; from which it should seem, that tournaments were introduced by the first Norman invaders.

[194]

G.H.S. del.

Etched by I.A. Atkinson.

Aquatinted by Hill.

A Tournament as practised in the XV Century.

1450.

note down the prowess of the knights engaged; and, in the middle, a herald, with the prizes, consisting of a helmet and a sword in his hands. Round the lists a multitude of spectators are assembled to view the sport. In the distance is a city, and in the fore-ground one of the marshal's men with a staff to pick up the fragments of spears, drive out dogs, and prevent their running after the horses, which might occasion their swerving from their line of gallop.

AUTHORITIES

The knight, in the centre, is from Rouse, a MS. in the Cotton Library, marked Julius E. IV. He represents Richard, Earl of Warwick, when he tilted in the armorial bearings of Haunslape. The attendants from the same and from the MS. copies of Froissart, in the Harleian Library, marked 4379, 4380, &c. Crimson pavilions from the same. Heralds, trumpeters, and judges from Rouse *ut supra*. The sovereign and his canopy from *Les Gestes des Rois de France*, in the Royal Library, B.M. The marshal's man *ut supra*. The whole has been thrown together in a kind of composition, because all the original illuminations are confined to parts only, of the field, and are all out of perspective.

A FISHERMAN.

ANNO 1450.

In the delineation of ancient costumes, the habits of the superior orders of society naturally claim the principal place. They are not only the most interesting on account of their connection with history, but they are also the most frequently described and represented. Of the lower orders of society it may be established as a general principle, that they dressed at a humble distance in imitation of their superiors; with the exception, that superfluous ornaments, or materials, were sacrificed to convenience. If we omit the hood, the dress of the figure before us is almost modern. He wears the fisherman's boots and the red baize frock, shortened round the waist by being tied up with a belt.

It may, perhaps, not be amiss to mention in this place, that the tools of almost all the ordinary trades have undergone little or no variation for the space of some centuries. In MSS of the middle of the thirteenth century, I have found, not only the trowels, spades, pick-axes, rules and squares, plummets, dividers, saws and hammers, but likewise the windlas, the capstern, and the pully. Indeed it was impossible for people who could build such bold and lofty structures in stone as many of our churches and castles, and could erect and transport the unwieldly battering towers to be used in sieges, not to possess a very considerable degree of skill in the mechanical professions. The implements of husbandry are still more ancient and numerous: Anglo-Saxon MSS attest, that the plough, (single and double-handled) the pitch-fork, rake, scythe and sickle, were in use before the Conquest, and have undergone little alteration.

AUTHORITY.

From a MS in the Harleian Library, B.M., marked 2838.
Below are tools and implements of masons.

A Fisherman 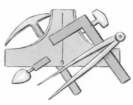 *of XIV Century*

1450.

ARTILLERY, WARLIKE MACHINES, AND SOLDIERS.

ANNO 1450—1500.

In a former number we have represented the earliest specimens of Artillery, which can be found in illuminated MSS. at the British Museum. These before us are taken from similar materials, but posterior in date by about half a century: they shew, that in the search after improvement, though the forms varied, no very beneficial alteration had yet been discovered. Indeed, as no fixed principles of science directed the exertions of ingenuity, mechanical engineers were bewildered by a multitude of effects, of which they scarce guessed the causes. The reign of Louis XII. of France had nearly elapsed before guns were made portable, and it required sixty years more, and all the patronage the great mind of the Emperor Charles V. could bestow, to acquire any satisfactory ideas relative to their calibres or dimensions.

The piece of ordnance in the foreground is fixed on the swivel principle, being suspended between the branches of an enormous fork of iron, shaped at top like a pruning-hook or hedger's bill: the cascable is perforated by a large iron-bar in the form of a scythe, standing in a vertical position, and terminating at top in a kind of hook, by means of which it is connected with the afterpart of the fork; upon this bar the elevation or depression of the gun is regulated, by means of holes placed at certain distances, through which passes a pin, or stopper. The whole apparatus is fixed in a strong iron plate fastened down upon a heavy bed of solid oak.

In the distance is another gun of a different construction, much smaller and lighter; it may be considered as a kind of field piece.

On the other side of the plate is a moveable tower, taken from an elegant and accurate illumination. It is a huge frame of timber placed on small rollers; open from the first floor downwards, probably for the convenience of moving with greater facility: from the height of what appears to be about ten feet, it is boarded vertically, with the boards perforated at a certain distance by triangular loop-holes for shooting or casting missiles. The top is embattled with embrasures, each furnished with a lid or shutter. Two upright timbers issue out of the centre of the tower, by means of which a large bridge is suspended in the air, with the foremost edge inclined like a roof, to serve the purpose of an immense pavis or mantlet, and protect the soldiers stationed on the battlements from the arrows of the besieged. These uprights were constructed so as to be capable of dropping jointly forward in the two foremost embrasures of the tower, while by some mechanic power the bridge was, at the same time, poised in an horizontal direction, and projected upon the ramparts of the besieged; then the men at arms, who hitherto had stood inactive, protected by the impending surface of the bridge, rushed forward on the enemy's battlements, and carried the town by storm.

The groups of figures are copied from several illuminations belonging to different periods, of the last years of King Henry VI. and of the reigns of Edward IV. and Henry VII. The foot soldiers are distinguished by the red cross of

C.H.S. del.

Aquatinted by J. Hill.

Soldiers & Cannon of the latter end of the 14th & beginning of the 15th Centuries.

Pub. Dec.r 1.1811. by colnaghi & c.o 23 Cockspur Street. London.

England on the breast and back. A kind of uniformity in the clothing, or at least some distinguishing marks, by which nations at war might know one another, and recognise friends from foes, most probably originated in times of the remotest antiquity. When John Lyon, the turbulent chief of the people of Ghent, advises his fellow citizens to resort to rebellious measures, he reminds them of an *ancient* practice by which they are to know each other, namely the wearing of white hoods.* By an ordinance of Charles VII., King of France, all the archers of the men at arms were enjoined to wear cassocks of the livery of their captains, which livery was always to be of the colour of their ensigns.† During the wars of the roses the English wore badges; thus, King Edward IV., his men had a sun of gold in a red field, those of the Earl of Warwick, a silver bear and ragged staff; the Earl of Oxford, the silver mullet (or star) on a red ground. At the battle of Bosworth the Duke of Norfolk's men wore jackets of his livery,‡ and those of Sir John Savage,§ for the opposite party, had coats and hoods of white.

But the most ancient cognisance, was that brought from Palestine, which, though at first common to all the Christian nations, the English in the end assumed to themselves; it was white, with a plain red cross. If it be permitted to resort to conjecture, in order to account for the introduction of this national uniform, we shall find the most rational supposition to be, that the banners of the city of London being originally white, with a red cross, the bands of infantry which belonged to the city had the same cognisances on their armour. As London furnished the largest and the most efficient body of archers, it is probable, that they were retained for a more extensive period of service in France, and that their celebrity gradually introduced the custom of clothing all the national infantry in the same manner, though the colour of the coat was not always attended to. There are many illuminations still extant in the British Museum where green and blue jackets with red crosses are almost as common as the white. In a splendid representation of Richard II. surrendering his crown to the Duke of Lancaster, two soldiers are seen one in blue with a red cross, in the character of a guard over the imprisoned king, another in white, with a red cross, as an attendant (probably a Londoner) on the Duke.

The English affecting a red cross, it was natural for the French to select the opposite colour, white. Thus we find that at an early period they wore white scarfs, and in the time of Philip de Commines, the Parisians wore red jackets with white crosses. Other nations had also their particular crosses. The Flemings bore green, and after the House of Burgundy acquired the Earldom of Flanders, a saltier raguly *gules* on a field *argent*. The Germans *argent* a cross *sable*. The Navarrese *gules* a saltier raguly *or*. The Scots *azure* a saltier *argent*. The Spaniards *argent* a cross fleury fitchee *gules*. The Portuguese . . . a cross *sable*. The Hungarians *gules* a patriarchal cross *argent*. The Danes the cross of Dannebrog, &c.

* Vide Froissart, Chapter XX.
† See Pere Daniel, Histoire de la Miliee Française, Vol. I. page 341.
‡ Vide the Letter from the Duke, quoted by Sir John Fenn.
§ See the Battle of Bosworth, by Hutton, page 51.

AUTHORITIES.

The piece of Artillery in the fore-ground, and Tower, from the Royal Library, B.M. 14, E.IV., Chronique d'Angleterre, written in the reign of King Edward IV., and the figures from Vespasian A. VII. and other MSS. In the back-ground is a distant view of Holt Castle.

PAGES AND VALETS IN THE REIGN OF EDWARD IV.

ANNO 1475.

The youths represented in the Plate are of the class of attendants on the persons of the great which the French simply denominated *valets*, to distinguish them from the menials then called *gros-valets*. Those who waited on the ladies obtained the name of *daimoiseaux*; and the ancient romances often recur to the services and intrigues of these handsome young servants. According to the system of education then in vogue, the children of the first families served in this capacity, and passed from their seventh to their fourteenth years as pages, and from that period to their twenty-first as valets, unless their strength and ability enabled them sooner to become esquires; from whence they rose to the high dignity of knight. Froissart gives repeated instances even of knights serving their superiors or parents; and we find the Black Prince twice attending on the person of his captive as a servant. But in the latter end of the fifteenth century, the vigour of the chivalrous institutions had declined, and we meet with a more effeminate system gaining ground: instead of learning the useful exercises of their ancestors, the young men of rank dwindled into fops, and from the scented atmosphere of a lady's bower, they burst suddenly into notice, as accomplished knights at some tournament where the prizes were no longer the reward of skill and valour, but of favour.*

AUTHORITIES.

The two pages in front, from a beautiful illuminated MS. in the British Museum, marked 15, D.I. The figure on the steps and portico, from Strutt, marked Royal 15, D.I.

* See the romance of Petit Jean de Saintré, and the life of Chevalier Bayard. The former was written about the time the latter commenced his career: and both give a correct view of the manners and customs of the times.

C.H.S del.

Etch'd by I.A.Atkinson

Aquatinted by I.Hill.

Costumes of
in the reign of

River's
147ß

Pages &c Valets,
King Edward the 4th.

A WARDER, OR PORTER.

ANNO 1480.

Among the most prominent in the domestic establishment of our ancient castles was the warder or porter.* As the office was of great importance and trust, it was never conferred but on men of approved fidelity and considerable personal strength. Hence the romances of the chivalrous ages have often transformed them into grim giants, who guard with inflexible severity the persons of young and captive damsels in the gloomy dungeons of their castles. The habitation of the porter was usually in a small cell, immediately next the guard-room, and under the main archway of the principal gate. As the drawbridge and portcullis were entrusted to the care of the soldiers on guard, or to the inferior warders, so the gate itself was reserved to the porter's own hands. By day he viewed the country from the drawbridge, or barbican, and by night, when the gate was locked and the keys deposited in the hands of the lord or governor of the castle, he ascended to the battlements, or to a small gallery over the archway; and from thence observed the vicinity, and, in cases of danger, blew his horn to rouse the garrison. Besides these precautions the jealous porter likewise kept blood-hounds, ban-dogs or mastiffs, near his person, and often interposed the well trained vigilance of brute instinct, where the service of reason was suspended by fatigue or obliterated by intoxication.

In the illuminations, representing the person of a warder or porter, few are observed wearing defensive armour. The keys and enormous club are the usual ensigns of the office: the horn is not so commonly attached to him, and, indeed, it is probable that in England, as well as in Germany, the alarm-horn was often fastened by an iron chain to some commanding part of the battlements above the gateway.† The specimen before us represents one looking out from the gate of the barbican. The original is destitute of colouring, and wants the horn and dagger: these are added from another. The back-ground is taken from fancy.

AUTHORITY.

The porter from the MS. of Rouse, containing the life of Richard Earl of Warwick, now in the British Museum, marked Cotton, Julius E. IV.

* Warder, wardour, Saxon, *dure-weard*, door-warder, porter, *portier*, *gardeporte*. The word is of Teutonic origin both in English and French. Originally the porter or dure-weard had the sole charge of the gate; but by degrees assistants, and then regular guards were appointed. Hence *watch* and *ward*.

† The horns are still to be seen in some castles of Hungary, and I have been assured, that in the same kingdom, a smaller horn fastened to a post on the outside of the ditch, for the service of benighted travellers, was still occasionally used within the memory of the present generation.

C.H.S delt.   Etch'd by I.A.Atkinson   Aquatinted by I.Hill

A Warder,   or Porter

H. Bourchier Earl of Essex.
1480

SHIPS OF THE REIGN OF KING EDWARD IV.

ANNO 1482.

John Rouse,* the Warwickshire antiquary, has left us some interesting delineations in his MS. of the life of Richard Earl of Warwick. Among these are several of ships, designed with so much accuracy, that they convey very distinct ideas of the structure of vessels in his time; and as they are repeatedly introduced under different points of view, each particular object in their conformation is successively represented. In these drawings, the eye retraces the origin of several names of parts, still retained in the marine vocabulary, although their primitive forms have so greatly varied, that the appellations bear no longer any immediate analogy to their present structures: such, for instance, is the forecastle, once built in the form of a tower, for the purpose of containing men at arms and archers; and the top, or round top, where the pilots were placed, a name expressive of its situation as long as the masts were not surmounted by any other spar. We perceive also, that the hulls bore some resemblance to the Dutch doggers of the present time, with the addition of forecastles and poops of such disproportioned elevation, as must have rendered these vessels very dangerous sea boats in stormy weather. When the fourth mast was introduced we have not precisely ascertained; but it may be conjectured to have happened about the period now under consideration, when sailing upon a wind began first to be successfully practised. The ships, being broad and full at the stern, must on these occasions have answered the action of the rudder imperfectly, and at all times steered with difficulty. Experience had probably pointed out, that this inconvenience could in part be remedied by occasionally employing more after-sail; and hence the fourth mast was placed almost upon the stern. It is upon this principle that the Dutch bylanders have a similar mizen mast to this day.

The specimen exhibited in the plate is composed of the compared delineations above described, and fully portrays the several parts just now alluded to. On the main-sail are painted the arms of the Earl of Warwick, and the top and pendant are ornamented with his cognisance, a bear and ragged staff. The practice of displaying armorial bearings or devices on the sails is of a very early date, and may be traced in the Cambridge MS. copy of Matthew Paris, where there is a ship with the arms of England (three lions) on the sail. Francis de la Marque, quoted in a former number of this work, represents the vessel in which Richard the Second returned from Ireland, with a sun of gold in the main-sail. We find the practice continued in the reign of Henry VII., and even as late as the time of Elizabeth.

In the waist, or middle part of the ship, are seen three pieces of cannon with their muzzles elevated, and the ports shut. The appearance of square ports in the sides of vessels, or on the gangways, is therefore not of so recent a date as Mr. Charnock seems to imagine. Froissart mentions cannon among other warlike

---

* John Rouse died at an advanced age on the 14th of January 1491, the seventh of Henry VII., after he had for many years been established in the chantry at Guy's Cliff, Warwickshire; consequently we may conclude that the ideas and sketches of his delineations are of a date some years earlier.

C.H.S del.

Etched by I.A.Atkinson

Ships of the Reign of King Edward the 4th. 1482.

implements, on board the Flemish fleet commanded by Du Buque, which was engaged and captured off Cadsand in 1387, by the English, under the Earl of Arundel. It seems the first trials met with so little success, that the French did not employ artillery on board their ships until 1494, when the Duke of Orleans, afterwards Louis XII., employed some in his fleet at the siege of Rapallo, on the coast of Genoa; although the guns on board the ships of Columbus, when he first sailed on discovery towards America in 1492, attest that the Spanish nation had already brought the invention to considerable perfection, before the siege by the French galleys above mentioned, took place.

AUTHORITY.

The MS. of John Rouse above quoted in the British Museum, marked Cott. Julius, E. IV.—Mr. Strutt has published fac-similes of all the drawings in his second volume of the Horda Angel-cynnan.

ENGLISH ARCHERS.

We will here say a few words on the subject of the bow, and the laws and discipline connected with archery. The bow required for the service in war, according to the best authorities, could not be less in length from nock to nock, than the height of the bearer, nor more than six feet six inches. Yew was the most proper material, though witch-hazel, ash, and elm, were worked up for that purpose. As the rough staves could not be procured in sufficient quantity, their importation was encouraged by several statutes and laws, which continued in force, until the improved state of fire arms, in the reign of Charles I. caused this victorious weapon to be finally abandoned, notwithstanding the opposition of custom, prejudice, and a recollection of the unparallelled victories, chiefly gained by its aid.

The arrows were of different weight and sizes; the lighter sort, for long ranges, about two feet three inches, while the heavy were a cloth yard in length. The heads had various shapes, among which the broad arrow extended in width to near four inches at the extremity of the wings. Of these twenty-four, in a sheaf, were put in the quiver, and, in action, about a dozen in the girdle. They were trimmed with three goose-quill feathers each, and when the archers shot in volleys, the quantity of arrows in the air and falling was so great, that Froissart, with a poetical turn of expression, compares it to the driving of snow. Besides these missiles, fireworks, and arrows headed with phials filled with combustible matter, were often shot from bows. The furthest range of arrows was estimated at about eleven score yards.

The archers in order of battle (at least at Azincourt, when their discipline was perfected), carried, beside the bow, axe, and target, a stake pointed at both ends. They fought in open ranks, and the files eight deep. When on the point of engaging, they advanced a few paces beyond the intended line, and fixed their stakes inclined towards the enemy in the ground; they then returned into the alignment, and from behind this kind of chevaux de frize, dealt forth their destructive arrows, and when the enemy was thrown into confusion, they sallied, and with small battle-axes, swords, poignards, and mauls, completed the defeat. Their reputation rose so high, that we see several princes in the 15th century esteem their armies considerably reinforced if they could obtain 2 or 300 English archers in their service.

AUTHORITY.

Cotton Library, Julius, E. IV.

English   *Archers*

of the Reign of   *King Edward IV.*

Willm Lord Hastings.

1482

N.º 23, Cockspur Street, London.

A LADY AND GENTLEMAN IN SUMMER DRESSES.

ANNO 1500.

These two figures are in the most fashionable attire of their time. The lady's dress is not unbecoming. She wears the stomacher, and the long, loose, and wide shift sleeves in imitation of the men's fashion. The gentleman's doublet is very short, and stuffed at the shoulders with waddings, called at that time *mahoitres*. The sleeves are slit to show the full shirt sleeves gathered in puffs under the arm. His *trouses*, or close hose, are connected with the unseemly breeches then in fashion. On his legs are slops;* and as the long-toed shoes, known by the names of *poulaines* and duck-bills had just disappeared, he wears slippers of the succeeding mode, short and broad before like a duck's foot; but not as yet so extravagantly wide as they became soon after (in France at least) when they exceeded a foot in diameter. His hair is long and flowing, covered with a small bonnet, ornamented with a button, and his hat, loaded with a profusion of feathers, hangs over his back by a broad strap. His pouch or sachel is richly embroidered and tasseled with gold.

AUTHORITY.

From a beautiful illuminated copy of the Roman de la Rose in the British Museum, marked Harleian 4425.

* Mr. Strutt conceives the word *sloppe* to be synonymous with short gown and paltoe; but we prefer the sense in which it is still understood in Holland, denoting a kind of spatterdashes (slopkousen) such as here exhibited on the plate. Indeed the names of garments, applied to the lower extremities, have at all times been ambiguous. *Hose*, in English, is applied to stockings; in German, to breeches.

Erthat by I A Atkinson

C. Somerset   Earl of Worcester
15 00

A Lady & Gentleman   *in Summer Dresses.*

SIR RHYS AB THOMAS, OR FITZURIEN,

KNIGHT BANNERET, AND K.G. GOVERNOR OF ALL WALES, &C.

ANNO 1500.

Sir Rhys ab Thomas, the Cambrian hero, was conspicuous for being one of the first to assist the Earl of Richmond in the insurrection against Richard the Third, by which the line of the Plantagenets was extinguished, and the house of Tudor elevated to the throne. He met Henry at Milford Haven,* accompanied him with all his forces, including a powerful body of cavalry, to Bosworth Field, and in the conflict proved himself among the most valiant in his cause. The Welsh maintain that he slew Richard with his own hands, that he plucked the regal diadem from his brow, and hastened to place it on the head of Richmond ere the shouts of victory had proclaimed him king. Certain it is, that Rhys, in reward for his eminent services, was the first person knighted on the field of battle by Richmond, now King Henry VII. Many honours were afterwards conferred upon him; he became Constable and Lieutenant of Brecknock, Chamberlain of Caermarthen and Cardigan, Seneschal and Chancellor of Haverford West, Roos, and Buelt; Justiciary of South Wales, and Governor of all Wales, Knight Banneret, and Knight of the Garter. Sir Rhys was the grandson of Sir Grufydd ab Nicholas, the celebrated patron of the Bards. He was born in the year 1451, and died in 1527 at the age of 76. There is a curious and valuable life of him, written in the time of James I. by one of his descendants, in the first volume of the Cambrian Register. By that it appears that he was twice married.

The costume represents the knight in his full habit of the Garter, with this singular circumstance, (if the original drawing be correct), that there is no trace of the garter on the leg. We have selected the figure from among several others habited nearly in the same style, on account of this omission, and because there is no engraved portrait of Sir Rhys that we know of in existence. As this brave soldier belongs more to the close of the 15th, than the beginning of the 16th century, it has been thought proper to date this Costume some years earlier than the time of his death. It is taken from a recumbent effigy considerably larger than life, on an altar tomb in St. Peter's church, Caermarthen.

In the back ground is a view of Carew Castle, where he lived, and where he gave a splendid tournament to his Sovereign. The present Lord Dynevor is the lineal descendant of this ancient family.

AUTHORITIES.

Monument on the North side of the chancel in St. Peter's church, Caermarthen. The drawing and particulars communicated by S. Meyrick, Esq. LL.D. and F.S.A.

* It is said that Richard having some cause to fear the power of Rhys, sent to remind him of his loyalty; to which he replied, that should the Earl of Richmond attempt to land in Wales, he should pass over his body before he invaded England; and that, to keep his word, he crept under Mullock Bridge while Henry crossed over.

C.H.S. del.ᵗ   Etched by I.A.Atkinson   Aquatinted by Flavel

Sir Rhys ab Thomas      *Knight Bannerett &c. K.G.*

Governor   *of all Wales.*

15 90

DATE DUE